Are You Up for The Challenge?

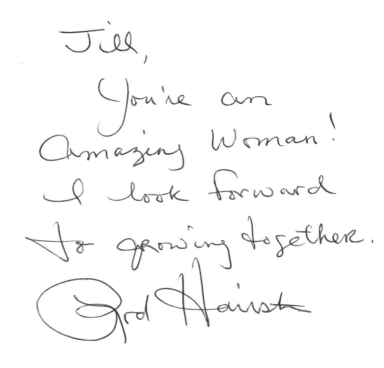

Jill,

You're an Amazing Woman! I look forward to growing together.

Rod Hairston

Are You Up for The Challenge?

Get What You Want In Your Life Starting NOW... Not Someday

By Rod Hairston,
creator of The 45 Day Challenge® Series

INVICTUS
INTERNATIONAL

Published in the United States of America
Invictus International
17014 Winning Colors Place
Leesburg, VA 20176
www.InvictusVision.com

ISBN 1-59932-016-9

Printed in the United States of America

Book design by Lighthouse Concepts, LLC
www.LHconcepts.com

TABLE OF CONTENTS

Foreword

I've been on a quest for many years to find a coaching system that is consistent with my philosophy of success. I have been invited by organizations all over the world to help inspire and facilitate change, and in the short hour and a half that I am with them, I am able to provide some of the impetus that inspired me to become the best in the world in the decathlon and a Gold Medalist in the 1976 Olympics. My message by itself is very effective. However, until now, follow-up coaching was the missing piece. I began to look for a model that would allow change to happen through commitment and consistency. I wanted a system that would facilitate lasting change.

I found that system with Rod Hairston and Envision-U. His 45 Day Challenge® programs have revolutionized the coaching industry. We have now taken well over 4,500 people through The 45 Day Challenge® system with long term, sustainable success. I am now able to deliver my message within a system that emulates the approach I took to become an Olympic Gold Medalist.

Not only will you enjoy this book, but you will also be able to take the 45 Day Challenge® principles and transform yourself into a champion in your own game. You will discover your hidden potential in all areas of your life: mindset, health and energy, relationships, and your career. Read this book with an open mind and believe one thing: The champion that lives in my heart is also in yours.

See you on the ceremonial platform.

Bruce Jenner

Introduction

I Took the Challenge

"I can't write a book commensurate with Shakespeare, but I can write a book by me."
— *Sir Walter Raleigh*

For years, people have been asking me to write a book. Some wanted the book because they heard about our Challenge Event and wanted to learn more. Some wanted the book because they had taken The 45 Day Challenge® and wanted to reinforce the positive changes they'd put into place. Others wanted the book because The 45 Day Challenge® had helped them turn around their lives, and they wanted to share these ideas with friends and fellow employees.

In the beginning, I was a bit hesitant. I thought, "Don't you have to be a Ph.D. to write a book?" Furthermore, I was busy juggling my speaking career, family activities, and community involvement, and I didn't know where I'd find the time to write a book. Then, a coaching client told me point blank, "Rod, I took your Challenge, now it's time you take mine. There are a lot of people waiting for this book. Make it happen!"

I took his words to heart. Part of the challenge is recognizing that life is too short to put off projects that could add value to your life and to the lives of others. If putting these life-changing principles into print could make a difference for even more people, then I needed to *make* time to write this book.

So, here it is. It is my sincere hope that this book helps *you* initiate and maintain positive changes that improve your quality of life starting today and continuing into the future.

How Do I Proceed?

*"There is no advancement to him who stands trembling
because he cannot see the end from the beginning."*
— *K.J. Klemme*

The principles in this book are taken from Envision U's acclaimed 45 Day Challenge® series, which has helped thousands of people create real and lasting change in all areas of their lives. You'll have an opportunity at the end of the book to learn more about The 45 Day Challenge®, to read a few stories from people like you who took The Challenge, and to find out how you can participate.

It would be a great idea to read this book with pen in hand so you can underline passages that are particularly important to you. Take time to jot in the margins how you're going to follow-up and use these ideas. An old proverb states, "A short pencil is better than a long memory." I agree. Making notes will help you remember what you've learned so you're more likely to put ideas into action and reap real-world results.

On your own, you can put the principles detailed in this book into practice immediately in any and every area of your life. At the end of most chapters, you'll have the opportunity to ask yourself questions that help you explore how these principles affect you, suggestions on how to apply what you've read, and key points to remember. And as your life changes, it's likely that you'll want to refer back to your answers, suggestions, and applications often.

Please read this book with an open mind. Give yourself the opportunity to grasp the timeless principles of this book. If you do, I'm confident you will see tangible improvements in all areas of your life.

Continue on, and let's grow.

How Does The 45 Day Challenge® Work?

Self-knowledge is the beginning of self-improvement.

— Spanish proverb

Let's Start at the Very Beginning

*"There's only one corner of the universe you can be
certain of improving, and that's your own self."*
— *Aldous Huxley*

Before discussing the "how-to" steps for improving your personal
and professional life, it's important to explain the psychological
concepts and behavioral laws that are the foundation of this
program. I also want to take a minute to explain a technique I use
throughout this book. It is the technique of intentional reinforcement through repetition and variation.

I usually deliver this information in live seminars. When I'm
standing in front of people, I can tell by their expressions and
body language whether I'm coming across clearly. It's easy to see
when they "get" what I'm talking about, as well as when they're
puzzled and need the information explained more thoroughly.
Since they're hearing this for the first time, I usually repeat important ideas and illustrate them with descriptive examples so their
"aha!" light bulb goes on and they fully grasp the meaning of
what I'm saying. This also honors learning theory, which states
that the more times we hear concepts in different contexts, the
more likely we are to apply them in our real life.

Since I want this to be like a conversation between us, I use a similar strategy throughout this book. So, right about the time you're
thinking, "He's said this before," please remember that I'm
purposely using intentional reinforcement through repetition.
(Yes, I did it just then.) I know from personal experience that this
technique can improve our ability to retain and recall this information, which is one of my goals.

What Are the Core Messages of The 45 Day Challenge®?

"If you don't run your life, someone else will."
— *John Atkinson*

Let's now look at the big picture ideas that are the foundation of
this program. Getting a sense of the principles on which this
program is based will help you understand the soundness of this
approach so that you can trust the process.

If there were three messages that are the core of the 45 Day Challenge®, they would be:

Core Message 1. Your unconscious physical and emotional habits are running your life — whether they are serving you or not.

Core Message 2. You unconsciously created your emotional and physical habits through committed and consistent thought, emotion, and action.

Core Message 3. Knowing how to consciously navigate through the powerful unconscious system allows you to create long-term habits that will guide you to your ultimate Vision.

You'll learn more about these as we progress. For now, just understand that these beliefs are at the root of everything I suggest.

What Are the Seven Big Ideas?

"People are always blaming their circumstances for what they are: I don't believe in circumstances. The people who get on in this world are the people who get up and look for the circumstances they want, and, if they can't find them, make them."
— George Bernard Shaw

There are also Seven Big Ideas that form the framework of this program. They are briefly explained below. You may think, "These are common sense." That may be true. The question is, Are they common practice? Just because we know something or agree with it doesn't necessarily mean we're doing it.

You may think, "I'm not sure if I agree with these." For now, please suspend your skepticism and operate as if they are true. While you are free to question any idea that contradicts your current beliefs, I'm hoping you'll do yourself a favor and give these a chance. Take 45 days to operate with this mindset and see what happens. I think you'll join the thousands of others who have reaped tangible rewards as a result of adopting these constructive philosophies.

A big part of this book is showing that people who blame what they don't like in their life on circumstances are looking for excuses. We're not looking for excuses here. We're looking for enlightenment. My goal is for you to understand what's been going on in the past that has been undermining your efforts to be your best self — and then to apply your new knowledge to create a higher quality of life and lasting positive change.

Big Idea #1: Know Who's in Charge

From the moment you wake up to the moment you go to sleep, you have two forces struggling to take charge of your life. These two forces are your conscious and unconscious minds. Your conscious mind wants to get better. Your unconscious mind wants to stay the same. Your goal is to learn how to enlist *both* minds to get the results you want.

Big Idea #2: The Four-Plus-One Life Categories

There are four areas of your life we focus on in this book because they have proven to have the fastest and greatest impact on creating and sustaining positive change. They are:

- MINDSET — The mental stance from which you view the world and your place in it.

- ENERGY — The physical stamina and spirit you bring to all your actions.

- RELATIONSHIPS — Your personal connection to self, family, friends, colleagues, customers, community, and your world.

- CAREER — The application of your skills and talents to work endeavors.

We then integrate these four areas into a bonus category of:

- BALANCE — A harmonious equilibrium among your many roles and responsibilities.

Big Idea #3: The Four Universal Laws

These universal laws aren't *mine*; they're agreed upon psychological principles that govern and guide our everyday behavior. They are:

- The Law of Control — Accepting responsibility for what happens in your life gives you the freedom and power to change.

   TRAP — Blaming others (not taking responsibility) keeps you stuck.

- The Law of Attraction — Thoughts and feelings draw "like-minded" opportunities to you. You pull towards you the things you dwell on.

   TRAP — If this power is unfocused or negative, it drags in people or situations that you may not want in your life.

- The Four-Part Law of Focus — Perspective produces reality in these four ways:
  - What you focus on, you find.
  - What you focus on grows.
  - What you focus on seems real.
  - What you focus on, you become.

   TRAP — Undisciplined thoughts drift to doubts and fears that can stall your life.

- The Law of Belief — Expectations shape outcomes. What you strongly think to be true becomes true.

   TRAP — Skepticism and cynicism become self-fulfilling prophecies.

Big Idea #4: The Four-Part Cycle of Performance

There are four stages in acquiring skills and developing new behaviors. They are:

- INCEPTION — Selecting a skill to be developed and beginning to build new behaviors.

- DECEPTION — Recognizing that what you're doing is harder than you expected. You are tempted to give up and retreat back to your comfort zone.

- TRANSFORMATION — Accepting the difficulty and persevering through challenges as you achieve incremental or major growth. From here you either drop back into Deception, or push on to Identity.

- IDENTITY — Incorporating the new skill or habit seamlessly into your life.

Big Idea #5: The Seven Categories of Deception

The hunger of our unconscious mind to stay put is so powerful that it invents seven possible ways to fool yourself into maintaining the status quo.

- The Victim blames people, fate, circumstance or bad luck. He says, "It's not my fault," and lacks accountability.

- The Rut Dweller retreats into routines and empty distractions. He asks, "What's on TV?" and lacks the motivation to raise his standards.

- The Certainty Seeker stays safe in secure sameness. He insists, "This is how it's always been," and lacks the courage to get out of his comfort zone.

- The Success Seeker is always looking for the next "big thing." He thinks, "Maybe this will work for me," and lacks the discipline and/or commitment to stick with things.

- The Pretender hides behind a mask of perfection. He insists, "I'm just fine," and lacks the honesty to admit he doesn't feel worthy.

- The Escapist hides from reality and puts his head in the sand. He lacks the ability to look at what's really happening in his life.

- The Stressed Achiever thinks status and financial success are the most important things in life. He says, "I'll get what I want, whatever it takes," and lacks humility.

Big Idea #6: The Three Essential Ingredients of a Habit

To form positive habits — that delightful stage in which we do something almost automatically and without thinking — we have to master the following three elements:

- Focus: Concentrate on a clear, vivid picture of the desired change.

- Self Talk: Select constructive thoughts and beliefs that support the change.

- Physical Expression: Use your body to create the emotion necessary to follow through with the change.

Big Idea #7: The Goal-The Ultimate Performer

You become an Ultimate Performer when you use the above psychological principles to your advantage — which allows you to harness the best of your skills, energy, talents, resources, and relationships to create positive results in support of your goals.

So, Why Is It So Hard to Change?

"Sometimes, when you look in his eyes, you get the feeling someone else is driving."

— *David Letterman*

You may be thinking, "I've tried to change before. I went to a motivational seminar and I left all charged up and raring to go. I was going to lose weight, be kinder to my kids, eat right, and stop procrastinating. And, it worked for a little while. Then, life caught up with me again, and a few weeks later, everything was back to same old, same old. Why can't I sustain my desire to be a better person?"

The first thing you need to realize is: You are not in charge, not really. Your true master is your habits, which are controlled by your unconscious mind. It really is a great system, if you know how to use it. That's the problem, though. No one taught us how to use the system-our minds-correctly. Isn't that amazing? Our unconscious mind is driving our life, all day, every day, and yet we're never taught how to make sure it's helping us instead of hurting us.

Think about it this way: say it's January 1st and you want to start getting in shape. You decide the best way to do this is to get up every morning at 6 a.m. and go running. Now, since you're a conscious creature who's made up your mind, that's what happens. Right?

Wrong. That's how you know you're not really in charge, because the next morning when your alarm goes off, you groan, hit the snooze button, roll back over and promise yourself you'll start tomorrow. Some of you might get up for a couple mornings, but then one day, you're particularly tired and you give in to the urge to go back to sleep.

Why does that happen? Your unconscious mind is just doing exactly what you've told it to do. "No, no, no," you protest, "I never told it to do that." Oh, but you did. Here's how: You've left your unconscious mind in control.

What Is This Unconscious Mind That is in Control of My Life?

"I used to think the human brain was the most fascinating part of the body, and then I realized, 'What is telling me that'?"

— comedian Emo Phillips

It's time to make a distinction between your conscious mind and your unconscious mind. Your conscious mind is your thinking mind; you control its thoughts and its direction. Its job is to reason, to think, to desire, to dream, and to want to be something more.

Your unconscious mind, on the other hand, ensures your existence by keeping your heart beating 24 hours each day, by keeping your lungs inhaling and exhaling, by keeping your organs functioning, your digestive, endocrine, and lymphatic system working...you get the idea. It does not want to change; it wants everything to function just as it always has. *This applies to your habits and attitudes in the exact same way that it applies to your physical body!*

Here's an easy way to make the distinction between your two "minds." Call your conscious mind by your first name and your unconscious mind by your middle name. My first name is Rod and my middle name is Erving. (I know, I know. I have no idea why my mother named me Erving, she just did.) So, my conscious mind is named Rod, and my unconscious mind is named Erving. Please decide what you're going to call your own conscious and unconscious mind.

In my life, Rod wants to grow, he wants to be better. He wants to expand; he wants to be courageous. He wants to help and support people. He is clear about who he wants to be. Erving, on the other hand, doesn't want to grow. He doesn't know good from bad, right from wrong. He believes "it" is working and his job is to maintain the status quo.

I can hear you asking: What is "it", and how does Erving know what "it" is and how "it" is supposed to work? Great question.

Your habitual ways of thinking and acting are "it" to Erving. They are what Erving wants to maintain. It is very important to Erving to keep those programs running just as they are. Erving's been watching everything I do from the moment I was born. He notices the actions and attitudes I repeat, and figures those must be "right" (or why else would I be doing them?!) so he makes them easier and easier to do. Erving doesn't know what is serving my growth and what is sabotaging it. He doesn't care. It's not his job to care. His job is to keep the conditioned patterns consistent. Just like he makes my heart beat 24 hours a day to an exact rhythm, he wants my physical and emotional patterns (habits) to continue just as they are.

Here's the kicker: your conscious mind programmed Erving to lock you into habits that don't serve you! Not funny, I know. What happened is, your conscious mind had no idea it was establishing lifelong patterns by choosing to repeat certain behaviors over and over. In other words, we train our unconscious mind without even knowing we're training it.

Once you understand this distinction between your conscious and unconscious mind, you'll see why it's so important to monitor how you talk to yourself. If you call yourself "stupid" or "idiot" when you don't perform the way you want to, are you hurting or helping yourself? It doesn't hurt Erving when I call him names and verbally beat him up, it only hurts Rod. It makes me feel worse about the part of me (Rod) that's trying to change.

If you truly want to improve, you need your conscious mind on board because that's the part of you that makes and keeps the decision to grow. You have to make sure to keep YOU strong by supporting your conscious mind, by not scolding it, even when you're not getting what you want.

Sure, Erving Will Cause a Ruckus

"What a man thinks of himself, that is what determines his fate."

— *Henry David Thoreau*

What we are going to do is teach Erving to help you rather than hurt you. Whatever you have decided to name your unconscious mind, you're going to re-train him (or her).

At some point, your unconscious mind is going to notice "you" are trying to change and it's going to rebel. It's going to come up with all these excuses for *not* following through with this "self-improvement baloney." Because your unconscious mind sees change as a threat to its survival, when you start doing things differently, it will immediately do whatever it needs to do to get things back to the way they've always been.

One of the many tricks it will play on you is to create a crisis and/or emotional urgency. You will feel compelled to take care of something that is "making noise" in another area of life. You must resist this false temptation to focus elsewhere.

Genuine personal growth and positive habits happen over time. Instead of being "*re*active" to what's in the moment and concentrating on what needs to be done now, be "*pro*active" and take action that will help you for the rest of your life. Staying focused on long-term results and the behaviors that will produce them is what you want your conscious mind to concentrate on.

This book is all about being proactive. Its goal is to help you take responsibility for initiating what you want in life instead of reacting to whatever problems show up (usually while you're complaining about them!). While it may not feel urgent to you that you complete this program, I insist that it is all-important that you complete this program. Doing so will shape every remaining day of your life in positive and powerful ways, and isn't that what you want?

Can I Change for Good?

"Do you think it's possible to change?" asks Linus.
"Sure," Lucy replies. "I changed a lot this last year."
Linus replies, "I mean for the better."
— from a Charles Schultz "Peanuts" cartoon

Lasting change is based on your ability to 1) determine where you want to go, 2) eliminate the habits that stand in the way of you getting there, and 3) create and integrate new habits that will help you get where you want to go.

The problem is that some of us treat our habits the way Linus treated his blanket. Linus was often wise when dealing with his sister, but he maintained one childhood habit forever. He loved his blanket. Nothing could make him let go of it. It was literally and figuratively his security blanket. He took it everywhere with him. No matter how dirty it got, Linus held on tight. I wonder if he'll show up at his college graduation with it.

That's what many of us do with our habits. We don't want to let go of them because they're what's known. They've become our security blanket. In fact, some people are more interested in being comfortable than they are in being successful. Once our unconscious mind grabs hold of something, it holds on tight. It doesn't consider whether or not this habit is harming us. The unconscious mind just knows that it's a habit and doesn't want to get rid of it.

How Do I Get Rid of Harmful Habits?

"The rats feed and breed by the hundreds near the
brewery. Grow big as street cats. And short-tempered!
They'll swarm all over you and hang on by their teeth."
— Sid Fleischman

There's a rather vivid analogy that can help us figure out how we can get rid of those unwanted habits once and for all: Think of a harmful habit as a rat. Can you imagine what it would be like having rats in your home? Well, some of us have rats in our heads!

For some of us, if we see something suspiciously furry dart across the room, we pretend we didn't see it. That's how some of us treat harmful habits: we pretend we don't see them. Other people jump on the table and scream "RAT!!!" and then call everyone they know to complain about the rat and swear they can't live in that house a second longer. Other people decide, "O.K., I see the rat, and I'm going to go kill it." They get their gun and start shooting at anything that moves. Some people rush to the store and buy the latest poison to get that dirty rat. This is like taking a pill to lose weight. "I don't need to work out, I'll just take this magic pill and it will do all the work for me," is the thought that runs through their mind. Some people become so worried about the rat, they have to self-medicate so they won't be so upset. They're hoping that if they get drunk enough they can block the rat right out of their mind.

Do you notice a trend here? None of those reactions get rid of the rat. The best thing to do is clean up the trash in your house (head) that is attracting the rats in the first place.

If the rat doesn't have any food to eat, he's going to leave on his own, right? Well, guess what you're going to be doing while reading and acting on the principles in this book? You're going to be cleaning up the mental trash in your head. You will give up complaining, blaming, and procrastinating — all the bad habits that reinforce unproductive behavior.

Your self-talk is going to be different; your focus is going to be different. You're going to be more grateful. You're going to treat people better. You're going to treat yourself better. You're not going to tell yourself how lazy or stupid you are. You are going to realize you are a human being with a unique set of gifts, talents and opportunities. You'll realize that no one can use those resources to make your dreams come true except you. No one can let them wither and die except you. It's all up to you.

It's Not about Impressing Other People

"There is nothing noble about being superior to some other man. The nobility is being superior to your previous self."

— *Hindu proverb*

I remember when I was in boot camp in the Navy. I tried to impress my instructor by doing more push-ups than anyone else. I had plenty of experience with push-ups because I'd been a wrestler in high school. I was in such good shape, I could do them with hardly any strain. When the instructor noticed how well I was doing, I thought I was home free. I was sure he was going to acknowledge how superior I was to the other recruits and go easier on me.

Much to my surprise, instead of complimenting me on my proficiency, he said, "O.K. Hairston, that's great. From now on, everybody else has to do 60 push-ups, and I want you to do 90. And, you all get the same evaluation. If they do their 60, and you do your 90, you *all* get the same mark."

That was an important lesson. Our instructor didn't want us trying to show off or impress one another. He wanted us to work from where we were to where we could be. That experience reminded me how important it is to always do our best (yes, even if we get assigned more push-ups!). If we give our all and try our hardest, we all benefit.

If you will commit to doing that, you'll see a huge difference by the end of this book. I know you're great now, but as my instructor taught me, it's not about being great now. It's about becoming even greater. And it's not about moving to your next level because I want you to, because your boss wants you to, or because it will be good for your family. You've got to do this for you. God's gift to each of us is the ability to learn, adapt, and grow. Up until now, many of us haven't taken advantage of this gift. That's going to change, starting now.

Are You Ready to Commit? — How to Lift a 3,000 Pound Automobile

"Take time to deliberate; but when the time for action arrives, stop thinking and go in."
— *Thomas Jefferson*

I'm sure you've heard stories about a 120 pound mother who lifts a 3,000 pound automobile off her child who's been trapped underneath. When that woman realizes that if she doesn't rescue her child, her child could die, she springs into action. As soon as she decides that car MUST come up off of her child because she loves the child more than anything, she is able to tap into reserves of adrenaline that allow her to move a car she would normally not be able to budge.

That's the power of commitment. People are able to do incredible things when they decide to act, when they cut off any other possibility. And that's what the word decision means. 'De' meaning from, and 'cision' meaning to cut off. Think about it. A surgeon makes an incision. I'm asking you to make a conscious *decision* to use the applications and principles in this book, starting today.

Want to make your commitment more concrete? Share it with someone else. Voice your commitment to complete this 45 Day Challenge® to your significant other, an advisor, a friend, or a trusted relative. You might even want to voice your commitment to someone who doesn't like you. That'll put some pressure on you. It's not that you are trying to please these people or win their approval. You are simply enlisting their support to help you stay accountable to your greater commitment — the one you make to yourself.

The last part is to resolve that you're going to make it through to the end. The power behind your decision is directly dependent upon the emotion you invest. The more emotional intensity you can summon, the stronger your determination. The clearer you are that you're going to persevere no matter what, the more likely you are to create the life you desire. So, get ready to:

1. Make a decision.
2. Make a commitment to someone.
3. Resolve to carry it through.

Please understand that resolving is the highest level of decision. It's at the level of expectation. Once you resolve that this program will work for you, you imprint this expectation into Erving. Once Erving understands this is an expectation, not just a casual interest, he'll help you take the actions that will produce healthier behaviors and habits.

Imagine you were given $86,400 every day. If your goal was to be wealthy, you would have to use that money wisely every day. Imagine that if you didn't invest that money or spend it on things that supported you, you would lose it. However, if you invested it intelligently, you would build a critical mass of income and be able to live off the interest for the rest of your life.

Do you realize that you are given 86,400 seconds every day? Do you ever stop to think how you're spending that precious time? Are you throwing it away on meaningless purchases or wasting it on frivolous activities that will not pay off in the future? Or, are you investing it and building a critical mass — your habits and identity — that you'll be able to live off the rest of your life?

The results you reap in your life are the interest paid on the critical mass you've built. If your habits have been based on success principles, you'll have a successful life. If you have not spent your time wisely, you will have developed destructive habits that will keep you from having a successful life. That is why it is so important for you to decide, commit and resolve RIGHT NOW that you are going to do whatever it takes to re-train your unconscious mind with these success principles. It is the key to building a bank of behavioral capital and attitude income that will pay off for the rest of your life.

Never, Ever Let Another Person Derail Your Determination

"If people could make me angry, they could control me. Why should I give someone else such power over my life?"

— *Benjamin Carson*

I remember when I was a Sailor of the Quarter while in the Navy. When I started out, I grew in rank very quickly because I was so committed. I got up every single day and did the best I could. I was excited about serving my country and had resolved to give 100%.

I had worked for several different people, including a high-ranking admiral, and had always received impressive performance ratings. That was, until I was stationed under a particularly difficult Senior Chief. Let me put it this way — my kind and his kind didn't match. No matter how hard I tried, we never hit it off.

Under my new Senior Chief, my marks started dropping. I thought this was a reflection on me, so I started putting in more hours and effort, but my marks still kept dropping. I worked harder. Unfortunately, as far as the Senior Chief was concerned, it seemed like I couldn't do anything right. After applying myself and not seeing any positive results, I got discouraged and decided, "I might as well start acting in line with my poor marks." My performance started slipping. I started coming in late and stopped caring as much. I told myself, "If I'm doing all I can and it's not enough, something must be wrong with me."

Then one day, a good friend took me aside and said, "Look, there's something you need to know. I go drinking with your Senior Chief. He told me he thinks your performance is outstanding, but he doesn't think 'stars' should rise through the ranks too rapidly. He thinks they should have their feet held to the fire to test their resolve. I'm telling you this so you'll know your marks are a reflection of his approach, not your performance."

That was a powerful moment for me. It showed me that I had been turning over control of my performance to another person. I had allowed my interpretation of what someone thought of me to side-track me from doing and being my best. That insight allowed me to go back to giving my all, no matter what marks I got.

As radio broadcaster Paul Harvey would say, "Here's the rest of the story." One day, the captain of our unit called both the Senior Chief and me into his office. He looked at my evaluations and said something like this: "Rod's been here for four years and he's always gotten great marks. All of a sudden, his marks are dropping. I'm concerned about why he is changing so suddenly. Senior Chief, I want you to look into this. Either we're going to have to put him in some type of therapy — or someone else is messing up this guy. One way or another, we're going to find out what's going on."

Guess what? My marks magically went back up after that conversation.

Can you imagine what might have happened if I had given up because I allowed someone's ranking of me determine my self-worth? Someone had done his best to mess up my programming, and for a while, I had let him do just that. Now I know better. I wouldn't let anyone have that kind of destructive power over me, no matter who they were.

Hopefully, you also now know better than to let anyone else derail your determination to be the best person you can be. My whole point is simply this:

**Don't worry about looking backwards
and trying to undo or redo your past.**

That's over.

**Focus on what you want and need to do right now.
Focus on where you're going in the future.
Stay true to who you are and who you know you can be.**

Which Beast Are You Feeding?

"Were we fully to understand the reasons for other people's behavior, it would all make sense."
— *Sigmund Freud*

My grandfather had a favorite piece of advice he loved sharing with me. He'd say, "There are two natures that beat inside your breast. One is vile, the other is blessed. One you love, one you hate. The one you feed will dominate."

The goal of this book is to help you feed and nurture that part of you that wants to grow to your fullest potential. Once you focus fully on that part of you, it will awaken and become the more dominant part of you.

I hope the first part of the book has explained, in a way that makes sense, why we sometimes behave in a manner that is directly opposite of how we *want* to behave. I also hope it's helped you understand how important it is to over-ride and retrain "Erving" so he's contributing to your quality of life rather than compromising it.

Hopefully, after implementing this system for the next 45 days, you will continue to feed your good nature — the one that produces blessed behaviors. The way you feed it is by loving yourself, appreciating who you are, having fun while you learn, focusing on how you want to be instead of how you don't want to be, and understanding that whatever you went through in the past does not equal the future.

Ready to learn the specific "how-to's" of this process? The rest of this book is divided into six chapters that represent the six steps to lasting, positive change. These are the same steps that people in our 45 Day Challenge® go through. Imprint these steps in your mind and understand that they are the key to moving from what is to what could be.

Ready to grow? Then, turn the page, and let's go.

Universal Laws and the Cycle of Performance

*I can't imagine a person
becoming a success who doesn't give this
game of life everything he's got.*
— Walter Cronkite

What Do We Really Mean When We Say, "I Can't?"

"Notice the difference between what happens when a man says to himself, 'I have failed three times,' and what happens when he says, 'I am a failure.'"

— S. I. Hayakawa

A lot of intelligent people (well, let's say they sounded intelligent) have told me we can't expect to change after we're 30. I believed this. I've tried to change, and boy, was it tough. But something kept nagging at me. I asked myself, "What's keeping me from changing? Am I possessed by demons?" Although my mother has accused me of that a few times, I don't think that's what was happening here. So what's stopping me from changing?

I've concluded that when people say "I can't," what they're really saying is, "I just don't feel like it." It's as simple as that. People try to change their behavior by doing the same things they've always done.

People keep on doing what they've always done, but each time they do it, they expect a different result. I've been told that doing the same thing over and over and expecting a different result is a good definition of insanity. I believe it. It stands to reason that we've got to start doing things differently.

The first thing we need to do is retrain the unconscious mind. You may think, "I don't really understand how to do this." Hang in there, because we're about to explain how we can use the universal laws we mentioned in the first part of this book to turn Erving into a friend instead of a foe.

Want good news? You can use a law without understanding how it works. You use electricity, right? You flip a switch and . . . let there be light! But, I'd be willing to bet you can't tell me how electricity works. Doesn't matter. It works.

I'm going to briefly explain these four laws because they are crucial to creating the quality of life you want. Scholars and philosophers have been documenting the effects of these laws for literally hundreds of years. They apply to every single one of us, across the board. That's why they're called universal laws. There are no exceptions.

The Law of Control — *Build the Village of Your Dreams*

"Once I get the ball, you're at my mercy. There's nothing you can say or do about it. I own the ball...when I'm on my game, I don't think there's anybody that can stop me."
— Michael Jordan

In seminars, I like to share a story that demonstrates the importance of taking charge of our own life.

Once upon a time, there was a group of people who were banished from the Kingdom of Ability because they had made too many mistakes. These outcasts and failures knew they had to build a new village, but nobody wanted to be the one to start; nobody wanted to risk being wrong again and looking like a fool.

At this same time, a lone traveler was making his way through the outcasts' valley. He was curious about all the people wandering around aimlessly, but everyone was so busy avoiding eye contact, he had trouble getting their attention, much less making a connection.

Finally, the traveler tripped a man crossing his path. As he was helping the guy to his feet, he asked, "Why are all these people wandering around this valley in the middle of nowhere?" The man immediately cried, "It's not my fault, I'm not responsible!" and dashed off.

The traveler asked someone else how they expected to survive the cold winter in the valley. The only response he got, no matter how or what he asked, was, "It's not my fault, I'm not responsible!" Now, this traveler, being a smart man, recognized an opportunity. He thought to himself, "Since no one else is taking responsibility, I will."

The traveler began organizing the outcasts and telling them each what to do. The outcasts were so relieved that someone was taking charge, they didn't question his instructions, even when they didn't agree with them. They simply followed orders and went along with whatever the traveler wanted. Before long, the outcasts had built a village in this valley in the middle of nowhere. There was only one problem. Everyone hated it. That is, everyone but the traveler. After all, it was HIS village.

What's the moral of this story? The traveler took responsibility and was able to create the world of his dreams. The outcasts gave away their responsibility and ended up living in someone else's world, a world they didn't like or want.

If I could teach people only one principle in life, it would be this one. When you take responsibility for everything that has happened and will happen in your life, you will be able to create what you want for your life. That's it. That's the Law of Control.

When you take responsibility for everything that has happened and will happen in your life, you will be able to create what you want for your life.

Are You Making a Movie of Your Misery?

"The reason people blame things on previous generations is there's only one other choice."
— *Doug Larsen*

I had a client who lost 3 million dollars when his partner embezzled from the company. I told him the first step to getting back on his feet was accepting responsibility for everything that had happened and everything that was going happen.

As I was giving him this, what I know to be, life-changing advice, he turned a scarlet shade of red and exploded with, "You sound like a #$##@% idiot! Didn't you hear what I said? *He* was the one who stole the money!" I asked him what had happened in his life since his partner ran off with the cash. He started in on his litany of problems — he'd been sick, he lost even more money, his girl-friend left him, and on and on. I told him, tongue-in-cheek, that he ought to sell the rights to his life story to Hollywood so they could turn it into a movie and he could make millions.

You see, I wasn't interested in letting his partner off the hook. I was interested in helping this man move forward. The way I saw it, he could continue to obsess about the money he had lost, or he could get busy earning more. The way for him to do that was to use all of his potential. He needed to take back his ability to respond. That belonged to him, not to his circumstances.

Have you had something awful happen to you? Do you find your-self weeks, months, years later still complaining about what this person did to you? Do you tell anyone who will listen how unfair or undeserved it was? Responsibility is not about blaming or figuring out whose fault it is. Who cares about what happened? The only question that matters is: What are you going to do about it now? Responsibility is understanding that we may not control what happens to us, but we do control how we handle it.

I get calls every day from people who say they want coaching. What most of these people want, though, is to explain why it's everyone else's fault that they have such a messed-up life. My Granddad told me a long time ago that **the secret to success is to be responsible for things you're not required to be responsible for.**

You create your world with what you think, what you say to your-self, who you choose to hang around, and what you decide to do. You create your world. Who cares what color you are? Who cares what you've gone through in your past? If it didn't kill you, it made you stronger. You have to take back that ability to respond, so you can start utilizing who you are. And, yes, sometimes people will do wrong by you. But you can deal with them when you are in control of your ability to respond. Taking responsibility means asking, "How can I get the most out of me? Who cares what someone else did? How can I utilize more of who I am?"

Someone once told me that forgiveness is giving up the hope of a better past. Forgiveness is the essence of responsibility. That means forgiving yourself as well. Forgiveness allows you to move forward and create the life you want for yourself, especially because you've created the life that you have now.

The Law of Attraction — See Yourself As a Magnet

"I keep the telephone of my mind open to peace, health, love and abundance. Then whenever doubts, anxiety, or fear try to call me, they keep getting a busy signal-and soon they'll forget my number."
— Edith Armstrong

Have you ever seen and felt a magnetic force? Think about the last time you attached a magnet to your refrigerator. Do you remember the "pull" that drew the magnet to the refrigerator and made it stick?

Do you realize your thoughts work like a magnet? They draw in like-minded situations and individuals who stick in your head. Even though you can't see or feel the force, your thoughts attract similar energy. The Law of Attraction says that you magnetize yourself with your thoughts. Whatever you send out is exactly what you will get back.

You will bring into your life whatever you consistently hold in your thoughts. The thoughts that you send out will show up in your life.

Positive thoughts will turn you into a positive magnet that attracts positive things. Negative thoughts turn you into a negative magnet that attracts negative experiences and situations. The thing about magnetic attraction is it doesn't care if you're attaching yourself to a bank vault (what you want) or to a trash can (what you don't want).

When I ask people, "What do you really want?" most people start their answer with, "Well, I know what I *don't* want..." Or, they'll say, "I don't want to be so exhausted," or "I don't want to be angry all the time." Unfortunately, that's how we've been trained our whole lives. We were taught to think about what we *don't* want, so this thinking becomes automatic.

If you spend your time thinking about what you *don't* want, that's what you'll attract: more of what you don't want. Instead of wanting *not* to be poor, you need to hold the thought that you *want* abundance. I know some wonderful, beautiful people who are good people and they lead good lives, but the majority of their energy is spent on what they don't want or what's wrong in their life. And guess what they get? That's right: more of what they don't want and more of what's wrong. I've been observing this for a long time and I'll tell you this Law of Attraction always works.

If you've ever played sports, you can attest to the veracity of this. If you are playing tennis and you tell yourself, "Do not double-fault," what do you think is going to happen? If you're skiing down a black-diamond slope and you're afraid you're going to fall, what do you think will happen? If you're playing a 3 par water hole in golf and you're telling yourself, "Do not hit it in the lake," what do you think is going to happen?

From now on, focus on your desired behavior instead of your dreaded behavior and fill your mind with what you *want* to do. Think, "I'm going to get this first serve in.", "I'm going to stay on my feet.", and "Arc the ball high and plop it on the green next to the flag."

The intensity of emotion behind your thought adds to the strength of the attraction energy. So, the more vividly you picture what you want and the more you ratchet up your enthusiasm about achieving your desired result, the more likely you are to produce it.

It's also important to understand that the intensity of negative emotion works just as effectively as the intensity of positive emotions. What this means is, your fear works just as powerfully as your expectations. So, be very careful about what you allow yourself to feel intensely about. Instead of saying, "I'm not going to worry about that presentation," say, "I'm going to walk into that presentation with confidence." Instead of thinking, "I'm not going to have a piece of that chocolate cake," tell yourself, "I'm going to keep to my diet and eat healthy." If you keep your mind firmly on the things you do want, you will set yourself up for success rather than failure.

Did You Know You're Swimming in a Magnetic Sea?

"Drag your thoughts away from your troubles — by the ears, by the heels, or any other way you can manage. It's the healthiest thing a body can do."
— Mark Twain

You also might want to drag yourself away from people who carry on about their troubles. If you hang out with negative people long enough, their problems become your problems. When you are in the midst of a group of people, you are sitting in a sea of their energy. Their energy is contagious-and that can be good or bad. If you're around people who are upbeat, focused, enthusiastic, and committed to making a positive difference in the world, their optimism will rub off on you.

If you're around individuals who are lethargic, bitter, resentful, or angry, that will rub off on you as well. If you don't proactively saturate yourself with positive thoughts and feelings, you'll end up drowning in other people's negativity. You will take in their destructive energy, send it back out, and attract even more back to yourself.

Remember the Law of Control? You are responsible for your life. And the way to create the quality of life you want, need, and deserve is to hold positive thoughts and send out constructive energy so you attract people, events and situations that will contribute to a good life.

The Law of Focus-Be a Magnifying Glass

"No steam or gas ever drives anything until it is confined. No Niagra is ever turned into light and power until it is tunneled. No life ever grows great until it is focused, dedicated, disciplined."

— *Henry Emerson Fosdick*

A magnifying glass can make small things bigger, and it can also make big things more powerful. For example, it can start a fire by focusing sunshine into an intense single beam of light. Focus is turning something diffuse into something with laser-beam intensity.

Focusing attention means aiming your mental energy in a specific direction rather than giving equal consideration to anything and everything that comes to mind. The results of focusing your attention are explained by the four-part Law of Focus:

1. **What you focus on, you find.**
2. **What you focus on seems real.**
3. **What you focus on grows.**
4. **What you focus on, you become.**

You may be thinking, "This makes sense, but how do I control my focus? Half the time, it seems like my mind has a mind of its own!"

Good point. The way you control your focus is to hold a picture in your mind of what you want. Vividly imagine it. SEE it happening in your mind exactly the way you want it to happen. Images demand the most attention from your mind. Whatever situation you're in, picture it going your way. Imagine your success. Visualize holding up a trophy, closing the deal, hugging your child, or walking into your newly purchased home. See yourself opening your own business, depositing a $50,000 check, finishing your book, or delivering a presentation confidently.

While you picture this perfect scenario, hold a word or phrase in your mind that captures the essence of what you want to have happen. Repeat that word or phrase over and over. You may say to yourself, "Play the music perfectly." "Cross the finish line with energy to spare." "Answer the questions with poise." The bottom line is that you want to fill your mind with thoughts that "show and tell" your ideal behavior so you can produce what you're imagining.

Focus on possibilities and on the compelling future you're working towards, instead of dwelling on doubts and on an imperfect past. Focus on growing and expanding instead of fearfully staying in your comfort zone. Focus on abundance instead of scarcity. Focus on what is right with your life instead of what's wrong. When you do that, you'll give energy to the things you want in your life, which will help manifest them.

If you don't consciously control and direct your focus, then according to the physical laws of the universe, chaos will direct it for you. Newton's 2nd law of thermodynamics tells us that any system left unattended will work its way towards chaos. Is that what you want in your life?

The Law of Belief-Break a Board on the First Try

"Believe there is a great power silently working all things for good, behave yourself and never mind the rest."
— Beatrix Potter

In my training programs, I've taken at least 20,000 people through an exercise during which they break through a board with their bare hand. Here are the facts: it takes only eight pounds of pressure to break through a board, and human bone is 11 times harder than the wood I use for board breaking.

Given those facts, it's obvious that everyone breaks through the board on the first try. Right? Not by a long shot. I've seen 200 pound men with bulging muscles hypnotize themselves into believing that they can't break the board. Whatever you feel certain about and expect to happen in your life will happen. That's the Law of Belief.

Whatever you feel certain about and expect to happen in your life will happen.

What's interesting is that you can tell just by looking at a person's face and body language whether or not he believes he can break the board. What you believe to be true tells your mind and body how to respond. Belief must come first, even before the "how." If you believe that you can break a board, I can teach you how to do it. But if you truly believe that you can't break a board, then no amount of "how" will get you through that board. You don't need to always know how to do something. That's not your job. Your job is to believe it can be done and then to act on the opportunities that are placed in front of you.

Believe big and you can be big, do big, and have big. I've coached a number of people who lacked initiative and drive. Most of them didn't believe they deserved more. My mission was to show them that if they believed they were worth little, they would receive little. If they started believing they were worth more, they would receive more.

How to Make It Out Alive

"Life is not easy for any of us. But what of that? We must have perseverance and, above all, confidence in ourselves."
— *Marie Curie*

When I was involved in special warfare, our leaders would tell us, "If you believe you'll make it out alive, then you'll make it out alive. But if the enemy can get you believing in death, you will get captured or die." It didn't matter what the odds were, they always told us that.

You may think, "Wait a minute. I buy into the idea that the more we believe in something, the more likely it is to occur. But in wartime — and in other situations where there are variables out of our control — there's no guarantee that what we believe will come true."

You're right. I don't mean to make sweeping generalizations, because there are exceptions to every rule. All I know is that I saw with my own eyes that what our leaders had told us often played out just the way they described. The guys who were consumed with fear often seemed to attract bad things. The guys who were determined to make it out were often able to overcome incredible obstacles to live another day.

Please note there's a big difference between *wishing* a thing and *believing* a thing. Hoping and wishing help, but they don't necessarily make things happen. Those emotions are too soft, too speculative, too wishy-washy.

You've got to believe. You've got to be convinced. When you have confidence in yourself, you always think "I can" no matter what comes up. Never sell yourself short. The size of your success will follow the size of your belief because the size of your potential is greater than any perceived obstacle.

Just Because You're a Fish Doesn't Mean You Can Drink the Water

"We are like a man standing in a clear stream while dying of thirst."
— Zen saying

If you were a fish, you'd get most of the water you need to live by osmosis. That's how you'll get these laws to work for you. You can't just read this book and expect everything to fall into place. You have to immerse yourself in these laws every day until they become a part of who you are.

It's not meant to be easy. It will take work on your part to train your mind and your body in new directions. Remember, your unconscious mind does not like change. Until it knows you are serious about your new direction, it will make use of every opportunity to put you and your thinking back to the way it has always been. You are going to have to consciously direct your focus every moment of every day in the beginning. After a while, the unconscious mind will take over and keep the new pattern running without as much effort on your part.

One more thing: your thinking up until now has created a certain momentum in your life that has to be re-routed by new thinking before new results are noticeable. You can't turn an ocean liner with one spin of the wheel.

Take responsibility for what you see in your life right now. Understand that you created your present reality by using (or mis-using) the Law of Control, the Law of Attraction, the Four-Part Law of Focus, and the Law of Belief.

Ride the Cycle of Performance if You Want to Reach Your Goals

"Everything we do and say contributes to what we become. We might not be able to identify any specific source because there are a multitude of facts. Every difficulty subdued, every temptation trampled underfoot, every step forward in the cause of what is good is a step nearer to being the person we have the potential to be."
— Dean Stanley

Everyone gets stuck sometimes. It happens. There will come a time in every relationship, every job, and every project where you'll ask yourself, "Is this really worth it?" The answer is "yes" far more often than you think. Just like everything in the natural world, your growth and change follows a very predictable cycle of four phases. When all the problems and the fighting and the disappointment come up, you are only in the second phase! Because people don't understand that it's all part of a larger process, they give up and move on to something else, or give up and remain stuck. That feeling of being "fulfilled" reaches full strength in the fourth phase, and you won't get there if you throw in the towel during the second phase.

The four phases in The Cycle of Performance are:
1. Inception
2. Deception
3. Transformation
4. Identity

Inception and Transformation are temporary phases, while Deception and Identity can be permanent. If you live in Deception you feel stuck. When you are living in Identity you feel fulfilled. The trick is that you can't get to Identity without making it through Deception.

Because you begin this cycle with every new adventure in your life, you could be in a different phase in each area of your life. You may feel completely stuck in your career (Deception) at the same time that you are excited about a new relationship (Inception), working hard at getting your physical body in shape (Transformation) and enjoying a solid relationship with your adult children (Identity).

Inception Is the Part of You That Loves to Start

"When people ask, 'What's next?' I always say, 'This is next.'"

— *Fred Rogers*

I once knew a man who wanted to write a successful novel. But instead of getting down to the business of writing, he would call his friends every other week with another big idea. One week he wanted to write a play, the next week a biography of his grandfather, the next week a reality TV show. Though he desperately wanted a big hit, he never actually completed any of these projects because he didn't have the discipline to follow through. He was addicted to Inception. He loved beginning a project with high hopes but abandoned it as soon as he ran into barriers.

I know a lot of people like this who will never reach their goals. They may be smart, talented individuals, but they are addicted to the idea phase of new relationships, new places to live, or new jobs. In a quest for these new experiences, they get stuck in a loop of Inception, instead of moving on toward the desired goals.

The Inception phase is that part of the Cycle of Performance in which you select a goal and start working toward it confidently. This phase is often marked with excitement and high energy. In the Inception phase, everything seems possible because your unconscious mind has not yet started its rebellion, real-life circumstances haven't gone wrong, and you don't have any resistance to battle. But you have to eventually emerge from Inception in order to be successful.

Deception Is the Part of You That Wants to Give Up

"All our resolves and decisions are made in a mood or
frame of mind which is certain to change."
— *Marcel Proust*

If you become serious about something you start, you will eventually encounter barriers and frustration. That's the Deception phase, in which you start wondering if "all this" is really worth it.

No matter what change you want to make, your habits are going to fight back. Your unconscious mind is not going to make it easy for you to change. That's good. You have to have challenges in order to change; that's what builds character. Where would life be without resistance? How could we build muscle without pushing against Deception? That is what life is all about: making it through Deception in the right way. But for goodness sakes, set it up so you can win.

Deception pops up when January rolls around and you decide, "I'm going to lose 20 pounds by June." Well, you've said that every year, and by February all the old excuses have reared their ugly heads and you've given up. Those excuses are just your unconscious mind saying, "Hey, if you keep up these healthy habits, you're going to change and I don't want you to change."

You *can* overcome this deception. Take going to the gym and lifting weights. Because you know consciously that being sore is normal and expected, you can work through the temporary pain of lifting weights. When Deception whispers in your ear, "It would be so nice to stop," you ignore that temptation and keep going.

In fact, the more Deception you go through, the more your muscle is going to grow. So even though you get out of bed with a stiffness and soreness in your legs and muscles, you still feel good because you know that the soreness means growth. When you're lifting weights and you get to the 11th repetition and your arms are shaking with fatigue, you don't freak out, drop the weight and say, "That hurts, I have to stop!" Instead, you grimace and grunt and keep going, because you know that the pain signals increased strength.

Physical strength isn't the only arena in which this approach applies; it's the same way emotionally, and it's the same way mentally. If you know something is good for you and it becomes uncomfortable, don't stop, put your tail between your legs, and run away. Fight through the Deception. Most people quit when they hit Deception. They remember the excitement and enthusiasm they felt in Inception, so they decide to start something new and miss out on all the rewards waiting for them in the next two phases of the cycle. Some people will stay in Deception and become masters of making excuses about why they are there. I'll tell you all about the excuses we use to justify Deception later in the book.

Don't Drop Out During the Deception Phase

"The secret to success is constancy to purpose."
— *Benjamin Disraeli*

You *are* going to go through the Deception phase. It always happens that way. Every relationship, every job, every career, has gone through Deception. You'll feel as if you've been kidding yourself or as if someone has deceived you. You'll want to give up and find something new that will really work, because this obviously doesn't.

It's not that you're lazy, or that the program/relationship/career isn't the right one. It's just that your ingrained habits are fighting back. Remember, the job of the unconscious mind is to keep things going exactly the way they are now. Your unconscious mind tries to "help" by holding onto patterns that make you feel comfortable, safe, and certain. You see, it's really no big deal. Your world is not crumbling around you; you do not always make bad choices. Understand that this is simply a phase you're going through and enjoy the ride. Call on your emotional muscles of determination, commitment, faith, and vision. Build them up so you move past this phase and stay true to your purpose.

Now I'm going to say something that may initially seem over-the-top, but trust me, it works. What I want you to do when you get to Deception is...celebrate! If there's no resistance and you can lift the weight easily, then you're not building the muscle, you're not growing. If you keep moving forward when you feel like you just can't do any more, you'll be able to build an even stronger muscle. I know that when I hit Deception I can get bigger and stronger if I push through the resistance. I know that if I keep going I'm going to make it into the Transformation phase.

Transformation is the Part of You That's Determined to Stick with It

"If you want to know your future, look at what you are doing in this moment."
— *Tibetan saying*

My wife and I bought a treadmill and put it right in our bedroom. We took turns and both started running. At one point, we got to the place where we didn't want to run anymore. But we understand how the unconscious mind works, and we knew that if we kept going at that point, when we felt the least like running, then transformation would happen. We knew we were starting to install a new habit. So we kept running.

When you keep going, it actually becomes enjoyable to do, and after a while it becomes a part of who you are. So, the third phase is Transformation. When you push through Deception and start really working towards your goals and dreams, you are in Transformation. This phase is all about persevering, especially if you don't feel like it. It's also where you start seeing results.

I had a client who was working on improving his intimate relationship. About four weeks after our coaching, I called him to see how he was doing. He said, "Fine." I said, "Can you be more specific?" He said, "It's going great, we're getting along, there's romance for the first time in ten years, we're communicating well and she's really happy." *I* was happy to hear that, but *he* didn't sound happy. And then blurted out, "How long is it going to last? I mean we're getting along great now, but how long before all the old stuff comes back? How long will we be able to get along like this?"

How interesting. You're getting what you want, but you're more uncomfortable now than before the relationship started changing. That's what happens in Transformation: you get a little nervous because change is starting to happen and uncertainty can be scary. I promise you that if you stick with it, you're going to start seeing changes. So when you are in Transformation, it's very important that you keep going and stay focused. Transformation is only a temporary haven; you can only stay for a little while. You have to keep doing what's working if you want that to be your future. You have to move forward or else you'll fall back into Deception.

What if Babies Gave Up?

"Do what you can, with what you have, where you are."
— *Theodore Roosevelt*

You're starting to acquire new skills, but you still have to work at them. It's all very methodical; you're doing everything consciously, so it's not yet a habit. This is called being consciously competent. You certainly aren't performing perfectly yet, but you are doing what you can with what you have, where you are.

Remember when you first started driving? Were you in some parking lot somewhere trying to guide your car or parallel park between orange cones? Your tongue was sticking out the side of your mouth, your knuckles were white on the steering wheel, and you were hitting all those little orange cones. You couldn't even look down at the radio. The instructor was glaring at you, telling you to take a left at the stop sign. You took a right. Were you thinking, "If driving is going to be like this, I quit!"? No, you kept driving around, listening to the man glaring at you from your right.

It's just like when a baby starts walking. The baby's walking around and you're thinking, "Oh my God! He's going to fall on his face!" You hold your breath and watch him teeter and totter, back and forth. What do you do when the baby falls? Do you grab him up and say, "Well, *this* one won't be a walker!"?

No! We don't do that! We understand that falling down is part of the process. That baby doesn't think, "I'm not going to try that again. I'm down and I'm staying down." No, the baby grabs on to the coffee table and hauls himself up and starts wobbling across the room again.

Same with us in life. We don't stop just because we fall down. We have to walk, because walking is a must. We want to learn how to drive, because driving is almost a must. Unfortunately, some of us forget to apply this lesson when we try something new or when we try to change habits. We give up when we don't attain an immediately perfect performance. We tell ourselves, "I'm terrible at this. I'll never be able to do this" and abandon our efforts. We get down on ourselves and feel like a failure.

It is crucial that we remember this natural stage of awkwardness so we don't give up when going through it. We need to remind ourselves that acquiring a new skill or changing a lifelong habit takes time — and persevere through this challenging stage when it seems as if nothing is going right.

If You Can Make It to the Bathroom, You Can Grow

"How do you find your way back in the dark? Just head for that big star straight on. The highway's under it, takes us right home."
— *Arthur Miller*

I remember the night before we were supposed to move into our new home. Our bedroom was littered with packed boxes, ready to be transferred to the new house the next day.

It was 3 o'clock in the morning and I had just flown home from Fiji. I had been up for at least 24 hours. I was exhausted, but I had to go to the bathroom. I had walked to the bathroom a thousand times in the middle of the night before, and I could easily do it with my eyes closed.

But this time, I got out of bed in my sleepy haze and kept bumping my leg and bumping my toes and tripping over all the boxes (unexpected obstacles!).

Now, when I ran into those unexpected obstacles, did I give up and go back to bed? No, I kept going. Did I get frustrated and say, "Forget this?" No. I wanted to go to the bathroom and I kept going to my destination despite those things that were in my way.

You see, life is about continuing to your destination (goal) despite the unexpected obstacles that get in your way. It's not about saying, "Well, I'm going to give up because I bumped my toe."

Remember this the next time you're frustrated because you're not getting where you want to go fast enough. Get yourself to the bathroom. Go! Don't let obstacles stop you when it comes to walking, driving, going to the bathroom, or paying your bills...because those things must be done. Do what you have to do in order to live the life you desire. Make those things happen. Don't make excuses. Don't sit around complaining about how hard it is.

Go. In your careers, in your relationships, in your goals, get to the bathroom. I don't care if you bump your toe. So what? Go get into the bathroom anyway. You've already bumped your toe. Don't let that stop you. You can't undo it. Move on in spite of it. Just don't quit. Don't let obstacles rob you of the life you deserve.

If you stay with your Vision during the Transformation phase, you will move into the fourth phase, Identity.

Identity Is the Part of You That Feels You've Always Done This

"I'd gone through life believing in the strengths and competence of others, never in my own. Now, dazzled, I discovered that my capacities were real. It was like finding a fortune in the lining of an old coat."

—Joan Mills

Pecos Bill, Paul Bunyan and Sally Crockett are the characters of tall tales. They have clear and unwavering identities. By reaching the Identity phase of the Cycle of Performance, you may not become a legend, but you will strengthen your identity.

I have a client who is a Master in a Korean martial arts school. He is in the Identity phase. Martial Arts is a part of him; it's a part of his being, of who he is. He is confident of his competence. That's where we all want to go in life.

You reach the Identity phase when the new actions you've been working on become your new habits. You have succeeded at changing your internal programming. This doesn't mean that you can slack off and become less diligent about maintaining your new standards.

Your old habits have been a part of your identity for a long time, so when stress or crisis hits, you may fall back into your old "comfort zone" for a while. If that happens, just make a conscious decision to stick to your new habits. One day you will realize that the same triggers that used to send you screaming for your comfort zone won't affect you at all. You are "finding your own fortune" and discovering that your capacities are real.

A great indicator of where you are in the Cycle of Performance is how confident and competent you are feeling.

- Unlimited confidence, unlimited feeling of competence: Inception.

- Lowered confidence, lowered feeling of competence: Deception.

- Average confidence, average feelings of competence: Transformation.

- High confidence, high competence: Identity.

Life 101

"Boy, was that a wrong mistake."

— Yogi Berra

Just because you know about the four phases of the Cycle of Performance, don't expect yourself to be able to breeze through Deception and Transformation. It takes work. It takes persistence.

Especially when your plans are not going as expected, be very careful about passing judgment on yourself. This is not "Beat Yourself Up 102," or "Here I Go Again Falling Down 103." Don't be too hard on yourself.

Some people welcome any reason to talk about themselves in a negative manner. "Oh, I'm so dumb. Oh, I'm such a klutz. Nothing ever works out for me." For no apparent reason, some people like doing that to themselves. They hit Deception and quit so they can talk about themselves and their rotten luck. They either like the attention or they get a lot of security or certainty from doing that. I'm not sure. But this program is not about getting attention or security for staying stuck.

Remember, the only wrong mistake is the one we don't learn from or the one that discourages us so much we decide to quit. The only way our new skills and habits become stronger are through consistent repetition, especially when we have to fight off the desire to give up.

How to Teach an Old Dog New Tricks

"Habits are at first cobwebs, then cables."
— *Spanish proverb*

There once was a man who lived in a bad neighborhood where there were a lot of robberies. He decided to get two dogs to protect himself. He trained them to bark and bite and protect his house. And the dogs did their job well. They did exactly what the man had trained them to do; they would bark and bite anyone who came into the yard.

Then one day, this man wins the lottery. The first thing he does is move to a gated community. "Ah! Here I feel safe," he thinks.

Now, do you think the dogs are going to say to themselves, "We're in a gated community, we don't have to bark and bite anymore"? Or, do you think those dogs are going to do what they've always done and continue to bark and bite anyone who comes near the house?

You know the answer: The dogs are going to keep on barking and biting because that's what they've been trained to do.

Should the owner go out and beat them every time they bark and bite? I can guarantee you that will only make the dogs angry. What that owner needs to do is retrain the dogs and undo their bad habits.

Your conscious mind is that dog owner, and your unconscious mind is the two dogs. Should you beat yourself up every time you do what you are trained to do (by the years of conditioning the old habits)? No. Be patient as you work on retraining yourself and undoing your bad habits.

Your unconscious mind is doing its job based on the conditioning you've given it in the past. Those thought cobwebs have become cables. Please understand that and be nice to yourself as you go about creating the kinder, gentler you.

Nice but Not Easy

"It's not what you are, it's what you don't become that hurts."

—Oscar Levant

Now, that doesn't mean you should go easy on yourself. You still have to be tough on yourself, just not cruel. Do you understand the difference? This is very important. You have to push yourself if you are going to become what you are truly capable of becoming.

When I was in the military, we had to go through some very intense training. We would give any excuse we could think of to explain our sub par performances and the instructors would respond along the lines of, "We don't care about your reasons! You're either going to do this, or be kicked out!"

They didn't care what we showed up with; their only concern was retraining us in a way that would best serve us in special warfare. One of the most interesting things I learned during that training was that human beings have access to ten times the amount of physical strength and endurance we are normally using. Your nervous system and your emotional and mental capacities are all superior to your physical capability; your spiritual essence and your mental essence are even more amazing. You have amazing potential in your ability to love, to be creative and to solve problems; in all of these areas you have infinite capabilities. Imagine how much of your emotional and mental strength you are leaving untapped!

When you meet resistance, you are simply experiencing that your unconscious mind is strong, and that is great news. The stronger your unconscious guidance system is, the harder it will be for you to change, but the harder that system will work for you when you *do* make the change. You can make anything work for you when you put it into the proper perspective. There is a Chinese Proverb that I really like. It advises, "The man who says it cannot be done should not interrupt the man who is doing it."

The Six Steps
of The
45 Day Challenge®

The future depends entirely

on what each of us does every day.

— Gloria Steinem

Create Your Vision

The significant problems we face
cannot be solved at the same level of thinking
with which they were created.
— Albert Einstein

You Already Have a Vision for Your Life — So Who Created It?

"He who every morning plans the transaction of the day and follows out that plan, carries a thread that will guide him through the maze of the most busy life."
— *Victor Hugo*

Can a missile hit its target if no one programs in a destination? Can it even be launched? No! The missile's guidance mechanism needs to know the destination. Think of yourself as that missile, and your Vision as the program that gets you to your destination. I know you're thinking, "But, I've never created a Vision for myself." When you do not consciously create a Vision for yourself, your unconscious mind creates one for you, and it's not necessarily the one that you want.

You are headed somewhere. In every category of your busy life, such as your career, your relationships, and your community involvement, you are following a plan designed by your unconscious mind. Everyone is following a plan — by design or by default.

This is so important to understand. If you do not deliberately create a Vision for each category of your life, your unconscious mind will do it for you. Maybe it will create the Vision from significant emotional events in your past, or maybe it will model your peer group, or the media, or your childhood beliefs, or your parents' behavior.

Does life feel like a maze? Do you know where you're going or does it feel like you're lost? If you don't know where you're headed, just look around at your life because your unconscious mind has already had to create a vision for each category of your life in order for you to function. Is that what you want?

Are You Playing "Let's Make a Deal" with Your Life?

"Life consists of what a man is thinking all day."
— *Ralph Waldo Emerson*

On the TV show "Let's Make a Deal," you can give up what you have now, a sure thing, for the promise of whatever is behind "curtain number three." Sometimes it's a new car, but most of the time, it's a herd of goats.

That's how some people live their life. They take risks by taking for granted what they have now and taking a chance on some hoped-for better future. Unfortunately, much of the time what's behind "curtain number three" is not what they wanted. They end up wasting valuable time or throwing away their good health or their loved ones-for nothing.

That's why it's so important to create a Vision of exactly what you want. It means you know what you're trading for so you're not wasting your valuable resources. I can hear you saying, "What if I write a Vision down and don't know how to get it done?" But it's not about how at this point. Right now the Vision compels you to develop the belief and the faith that sets everything into motion. First you believe, THEN you'll see.

I have a friend and client who is the chairman of the most successful online mortgage company in the world. He borrowed $5,000 13 years ago and has turned that initial capital into a fortune worth at least $600,000,000. He created such a supportive environment for the 2,000 people in his company that Fortune magazine listed his company as the twelfth best place to work. If anyone asks him how he did it he says, "You'll see it when you believe it, not before."

In order to make anything happen, you have to have something to believe in. The how comes later. You'll be amazed at what you draw into your life. You have to start with the Vision, though. You have to! And you have to make it big, you have to make it bright, you have to allow it to give energy to you and to your life. You can always change it, but it's time to wake up and realize that you're in the game, so you might as well play. To paraphrase Emerson, "Life consists of what a man is *believing* all day."

It's time now to start living and stop letting your automatic patterns hold you back. It's time to expand and design a world the way you want it to be. And hopefully, your world will promote happiness, not just for you, but for everyone who has the opportunity to be around you. Let your life be an example of achievement and growth.

Following your Vision will also help you be an example of what is possible so that other people can see that life is about creating and adding to mankind, not taking away. Without a Vision, we're prone to adopt an attitude of scarcity, the thinking that says life is a win-lose game. If you win, I lose; if I win, you lose. A fulfilled life is not about that type of mentality at all. It is about the understanding that you create your life based on the Vision that you hold.

How to Build a Functional House

"We are what we think. All that we are arises with our thoughts."
— Buddha

You want to create a Vision for your life because you are a co-creator of everything that happens to you. That means that you are co-responsible for creating your life.

If I wanted to build a house, how could I build it without knowing what I wanted it to look like? Where would I build the foundation? When would I know when I was finished? How would I know where to put the doors? How would I know where to put the rooms, and how would I be able to make it functional? I have to have a blueprint to make my house functional.

How can I make my life functional? For my life I have to have a Vision. I have to know where I want to go so I can start moving there. It's not about what I get; it's about who I become. So your Vision will allow you to chart your growth, to measure who you're being, and to measure who you're becoming. It will also give you the opportunity to stop being the person you don't want to be. That's what your Vision is for.

You create your world. I'm telling you this as an absolute truth, and I think a lot of times we miss that. You create your world. You create your life. And in fact, the most successful people in our world are always creating, whether it's new products, new perspectives, or new paradigms. They don't compete, they create. They create things that vastly change our world. They create things we need that weren't here before. These are the wealthiest people in our world.

Your 747 Guidance System

"Let our advance worrying become advance planning."
— Winston Churchill

The rest of us have to be the same way. We have to realize that we are responsible for creating what we want in every area of our life. I chose four areas in this book to build a strong foundation for your life: mindset, health, relationships, and career. So, when you know you are a co-creator, you understand that you need to write out your plans before you build your house, or your life.

Another reason you must consciously create a Vision is that you may want to improve on the one you've already created unconsciously. In every area of your life, you have a current Vision: for your finances, you have a Vision; in relationships, you have a Vision; in health and energy, you have a Vision; for your career, you have a Vision for your spirituality, you have a Vision.

How do I know? Because, the unconscious mind is made that way. It's a guidance mechanism. Remember that you are like a 747 jumbo jet. If you don't put a destination into the computer, the jet won't start. It needs to gauge how much fuel it needs and how to stay on course. In short, the jet will not take off unless it has a destination.

Every day of your life, you are taking off somewhere and creating something. Do you know where you are going and what it is you're creating? Look around you and you'll have a good idea where you're headed. Your unconscious mind is very sophisticated, more sophisticated than any computer out there, and it has to have a clear-cut Vision of where you want to go and how you want to grow.

If you don't consciously create images of what you want, you will probably create images of what you don't want. You're even more likely to do this when emotional urgency descends, and it always will. If you don't know what you want, then you'll end up focusing on what you don't want. This is what we do when we worry about things.

So you must understand that if you don't use your imagination, it will use you. In order for you to focus on what you want, you have to know what you want. You must know. If you don't know what you want, you'd better make a decision now. Why? Because, if you don't know what you want, then you can't focus on it consciously.

Remember, your unconscious mind needs direction in order to function. Focus is just disciplined imagination. So if you don't know what you want, sit down tonight and make a decision. You must make a conscious decision about where you want your life to go. Make a decision now so that you can start controlling your thoughts and creating a Vision for yourself.

Your Vision Is the Sun of Your World

"Going blind. Sounds like a fate worse than death, doesn't it? Seems like something which would get a little kid down. Well I'm here to tell you that it didn't happen that way — at least not to me."

— *Ray Charles*

Remember the Law of Control? You have the ability to change the direction of your unconscious mind, and the first step is to consciously create a compelling Vision for each area of your life. Let your Vision be big, bold, and bright. Let it take you outside your comfort zone.

Your Vision is to your life as the Sun is to the Earth. The Sun sustains life on Earth. All the plants and trees move towards the Sun, because it helps to give them life. The Sun is a long way away and we'll never reach it. But, like plants and flowers, we keep turning towards it. Why? Because it sustains life. That's what your Vision can do for you. When you deliberately create a Vision for your life, you are able to turn from the mistakes of the past and look forward.

Your Vision will remind you of where you are going so that you can create the proper attitudes, the proper strategies, the proper beliefs, the proper goals, and the proper communication to fulfill that Vision. That is what the Vision is for. You don't know if you are doing something good or bad, right or wrong for your life unless you know your Vision.

Your Vision will help you turn your head away from your past and look forward. You want to look into the brightness of your Vision and you want to move towards it. Like the saying goes, you want to move towards the light.

Start Inside If You Want to Create Outside

"When I was a kid, my fantasy life was my salvation...it saved me by taking me from where I was to where I wanted to be."
— *Rosie O'Donnell*

We have 100 million sensory receptors that we can use to experience the world through our five senses: taste, touch, sight, hearing and smell. However, we have hundreds of billions of brain cells that we can use to create. That means that our ability to create is one hundred thousand times greater than our ability to seek. With that understanding it's time to start building that image.

You can use your senses in conjunction with your inner world to create. You want to see every aspect of yourself being a certain way: feeling, tasting, touching, seeing, hearing and smelling. Leonardo da Vinci tells us to use all our senses when we create an image of ourselves, and to play with the images in our minds to create a world inside that will match the world we want to see outside. Because the world outside already matches the world inside.

So if you want to change your world outside, change your world inside. And enjoy the process. Be just as grateful for the things you receive in your mind's image as for the things you receive in your outside life. When you create your image, be just as grateful, just as loving, and just as appreciative as you will be when it happens in your reality. Create the attitudes you want on the inside first, and your world outside will reflect that.

Concentrating your power on your Vision is going to give you the things that you want. It's like holding a magnifying glass over a piece of paper in the hot sun. That magnifying glass will direct and focus the heat of the Sun, and it will create fire. It will burn that paper. If your intention is to burn the paper, then you've done something effective. If your intention is not to burn the paper, if you want the paper to be really safe, then you've done something ineffective: you've used a great tool in a counterproductive manner.

Again, it's not about your character; it's about how you utilize the principles. When you focus on what you don't want in your life, you're using a powerful tool ineffectively. Of course, there are going to be situations that happen in your life that you don't like, but you have to deal with them. Deal with them by focusing on what you want as a solution. Only focus on the problem long enough to understand it and to learn from it. The rest of your energy must be focused on how you want to resolve this problem in your life. Got that? That's very important.

Want to Play Golf Like Tiger Woods?

*"Imagination is the beginning of creation. You imagine
what you desire; you will what you imagine; and at last
you create what you will."*
> — *George Bernard Shaw*

Here are some specific instructions for creating your Vision:

1. It must be stated in the positive.

2. You must imagine what you want as if it has already
   happened.

That's it: two simple directions that I bet you would have figured
out on your own anyway. Remember that you always want to
focus on what you want in life instead of what you don't want.
That's what "stated in the positive" means. And when you are
writing out your Vision, use the present tense to describe exactly
what you want.

For example, you'd write, "I jump out of bed every day with a
huge smile on my face." You would not write, "I don't want to
wake up crying." You would also not write, "It would be great if
I could jump out of bed every day with a huge smile on my face."
You write what you want as if it's taking place in your life right
now.

Be very specific about what you want. Remember to engage all
your senses, and don't try to do it perfectly. I'm not talking about
creating a perfect Vision; I'm talking about creating a place to
start. You can always change your Vision after you see what
works and what doesn't.

As you practice seeing your Vision in your imagination, you want
to run a bright, vivid movie of yourself in your mind, living your
life exactly as you want to live it. It's just like Tiger Woods visualizing his golf game. He's telling his unconscious mind, "This is
the shot I am making." That's what great athletes do: they use

visualization to help make their game great. Remember that the mind cannot tell the difference between something that actually happens and something that it vividly and consistently imagined. So, by visualizing yourself living the life you ideally want, you are practicing being who you want to be, and you will reap the rewards in your life.

You have to discipline yourself to see your world as you want it to be, not to look at the gap between who you are and who you want to be. A Vision is about seeing what you want in your life as if you already have it, not seeing that you don't have it.

A person can say, "I really need that million dollars, I have to get that million dollars." You know, it's a whole different ball game to actually see yourself with what you want than to see yourself wanting what you want. When you see your life as you want it to be, you're not operating from urgency anymore, you're not operating from scarcity.

If you're looking for the car keys and you're focused on looking for your missing car keys, then you won't find them. They'll remain "missing." What I'm saying is, if I need to find my car keys, I'll visualize myself with my keys in hand, unlocking the car door and starting the engine. Then, I relax and my unconscious mind will help me find them. It's a whole different approach.

Enjoying the Journey Gives Energy

"I felt the way popcorn kernels must feel when they are sizzling."

— *Sylvia Peck*

Many people are hesitant to create a big, bold Vision because they are afraid of failing again. They don't want to set themselves up for another disappointment, for even further ridicule or humiliation. These people are completely missing one important piece of information: Life is about happily achieving, not achieving to be happy.

You've probably heard the maxim "Enjoy the journey." Like many clichés, this one is true. Go ahead and create a big Vision for yourself because the real truth is that it doesn't so much matter if you reach that specific Vision. What matters is that you are moving towards a Vision and thoroughly enjoying the process. I notice that when I enjoy what I'm doing I have lots of energy, vibrancy, and creativity.

Things that I do grudgingly, grinding my teeth all the way, often give me the results I thought I was after. But I'm still not happy. I have so many clients that have made millions of dollars and are saying, "Is this all there is? Maybe if I had even more money I'd really be happy." The story of the person going for the goal, ignoring all else along the way, almost always ends with a desperate questioning: "Is this all there is? I thought I'd be happy. Why am I not happy?" They were looking outside for something that they have to give themselves.

So be very careful. Life is not about making it through each day with your teeth gritted, straining your neck, thinking, "When I get that success, then I'll be happy." No, it's not about that at all. It's about happily achieving. It's about self-discovery and experiencing the true capability of your "self." Enjoy the goals you've set and everything you have to do to make them happen. Then you will feel fulfilled in your life.

Why Not Ski When Others Complain about Freezing?

"If you start worrying about the people in the stands, before too long you're in the stands with them."
— baseball manager Tommy Lasorda

Now, like I said before, there are certain things in your life that you will definitely have to deal with. You have to create your life with what you have. Your life is going to go through different seasons; life just works that way. The seasons are going to come. I can't stop winter from coming, but I can ski instead of freeze. Right? You might be in a different season in your life than someone else. That's OK. What you create for yourself with what you have in front of you is completely up to you.

Knowing and following your Vision is about happily achieving. It's about improving. It's about living. It's about expanding who you are. It's about realizing that you've been sitting on the bench in the game of life and finally deciding to get yourself into the game.

Life is not about feeling bad because of what you don't have, or feeling like you're locked into your unconscious vision. It's not about that. There are olive trees that have been alive for a thousand years and are still bearing fruit. That's what your Vision is; your Vision gives you energy to bear fruit in your life, to live, to be vibrant, and to appreciate the time that you've been given.

One more instruction: Even though you love your new Vision, it is not something that you run out and tell everyone about. If you go up to your friends and say, "I'm a millionaire now, and I have a Rolls Royce," they'll write you off as delusional. Chances are, they don't understand how the unconscious mind works and they want you to stay right where you are. That makes them feel safe. Unfortunately, not everyone will be happy about your success. Not everyone will be glad that you're determined to improve yourself. Don't worry about them, and don't let them bring you down.

So, don't go around screaming out your Vision for your life; you'll be setting yourself up for too much rejection, doubt, or interference that can hinder what you're imaging for your life. If you are fortunate, you'll have at least one person in your life you will want to share your Vision with. This is someone who will encourage your Vision and help hold you accountable. Seek out and enlist that person's support.

Try This at Home —
Questions, Suggestions, and Action Plans

To Explore

- Why is it important that you understand how the unconscious mind works?

- What will you gain in your life with this understanding?

- What might it cost you if you ignore how the unconscious mind works?

- Why is it important that you identify where you are in the Cycle of Performance for each area of your life?

- What will you gain by doing this?

- What will you lose if you don't do this?

- Why is it important that you create a Vision for your life?

- What will you gain by doing this?

- What will you be missing in your life if you don't consciously create a Vision?

To Act

- Start building your decision muscle by making at least one small decision every day.

- Mentally review your day: how much of your day was lived out of habit? Do those habits support you?

- Forgive anyone whom you believe has caused you harm in any way, shape or form. This is a form of taking responsibility.

- Each morning as you wake up, deliberately focus your mind on what you want to happen that day in each area of your life, including how you want to feel.

- Identify where you are in the Cycle of Performance for each area of your life (mindset, energy, relationships, and career).

- Write your own dynamic, empowering Vision for your life. Be sure to include all life areas.

- Focus on your Vision daily.

- For every emotional state (attitude) that you indulge in, ask yourself: Is this attitude moving me towards or away from my Vision?

- For all actions that you take, ask yourself: Will this action move me towards or away from my Vision?

To Remember

- Your mind functions perfectly; it's the conditioning that needs to be altered.

- Thoughts create reality; think about what you want instead of what you don't want.

- Don't allow circumstances to impact your standards. Maintain high standards for yourself no matter what is going on around you.

- The nature that you feed will dominate your experience.

- You create what you focus on, not the other way around.

- You will go through the Deception phase; there is no short-cut. BUT, how long you stay in Deception is up to you.

- If you persist, especially when you don't "feel" like it, you will be rewarded for your hard work.

- You are moving towards some Vision every day of your life.

- If you don't consciously create a Vision, your unconscious mind will create one for you.

NOTES

*The universal principles will never show up in your life
until you know they're there. When you believe them,
you'll see them everywhere.*

— *Wayne Dyer*

NOTES

When you have to make a choice and don't make it,
that is in itself a choice.

— William James

Break Unwanted Habits

*It seems, in fact, as though the second half
of a man's life is made up of nothing but the
habits he accumulated during the first half.*

— Fyodor Dostoyevsky

Your 90% Blind Spot

"If I don't practice the way I can, then I don't play the way I should."

— *tennis player Ivan Lendl*

Now that we have thought about Vision, it's time to start actively working towards that Vision. Your Vision won't automatically happen; you have to do your part. Ninety percent of what you do on a daily basis, you do out of habit. In order to break out of your 90%, you need to look unflinchingly at some of those habits.

During this process you will be re-training your unconscious mind. In other words, you will be developing new habits. These habits will help you get to where you want to go. Before you can start working on new, empowering habits, however, you have to make room for them by getting rid of those old habits that aren't helping you. You developed those old habits unconsciously to support your old Vision. They were probably helpful in some way in the past, but they're not going to get you to where you want to go in the future. You're not going to be the person you truly want to be until you realize that you don't have to keep all your current habits and patterns. To paraphrase what tennis champ Lendl said, if we don't act the way we can, we won't produce the way we should. Most of what we do habitually we got from somebody else anyway.

This was the case in an experience I had with my grandmother. A while ago, she gave me a 286-mhz computer. Since she gave it to me, I figured I had to keep it. Well, it was slow, and I was having a hard time keeping up with my business using the 286. Finding software that would work with it was impossible. That's when I decided to get rid of the 286 and buy myself a computer with Pentium technology. I still love my grandmother, and that 286 worked fine when it was made, but to get me where I wanted to go I had to upgrade. Realize that it's O.K. to change old patterns. You have to. Just make it happen.

Our habits are like the programs in that old computer. I picked up a lot of patterns from my father and my mother and my grand-parents. Many of these "inheritances" aren't serving me today. Those are their patterns, chosen for different lives in different times. So I thank my habits very much for bringing me to this point in life, but now I'm going to update my programming.

Hard to Start but Easy to Live With

"Your mind is only as strong as your weakest think."
— *graffiti*

I do 100 push-ups every day. Why? It's a habit. If I don't do them, I don't feel right; my arms don't feel right, and my back doesn't feel right. When I first met my wife, she commented on the fact that I never went a day without doing my push-ups. She asked me if that was hard to do. I remember telling her, "Good habits are hard to start, but easy to live with. Bad habits are easy to start, but they're hard to live with."

Think about your bad habits. Did you have to work to make them habits, or did they just sneak up on you? Eating sweets, watching TV...easy, right? We need to look at our habits, because most of what we do, we do out of habit. In fact, our attitudes and our emotional states are habits. Your emotional states control your thinking. If you ask yourself a question while you're feeling fearful, you will get a much different answer than if you had asked the same question of yourself when you were feeling courageous or loving.

How does anything become a habit? You create a habit when you repeat a behavior over and over. Simple as that. Whether it is an action or an emotional state (attitude), anything that you do repeatedly will become a habit. You have to be careful about what emotions you allow yourself to live in every day. Your resolve is only as strong as your weakest thought — so make sure you focus only on thoughts and actions that help you be your best.

You Only Have to Salivate If You're a Dog

"If you are a dog and your owner suggests that you wear a sweater...suggest that he wear a tail."
— *Fran Lebowitz*

One of the things I really enjoyed learning about in college was the story of Pavlov's dogs. Pavlov was a behavioral psychologist, and he would ring a bell every time he fed his dogs. He'd wait until the dogs were really hungry, then he'd ring the bell and give them food. Ring the bell and give them food. Over and over again, whenever they were really hungry. The food would make the dogs salivate (I guess it was good food, or maybe the dogs were just really hungry).

The bell, of course, meant nothing, but the dogs figured out that when the bell rang they would get food. So, every time the bell rang, the dogs would salivate because they knew that food was coming. After a while, whenever the bell rang the dogs would salivate whether there was food or not. The bell would ring, they would start salivating. Salivating had become a habit triggered by the sound of the bell. It had become a trained, conditioned response.

Are there any bells in your life that make you salivate? There are probably things you do and feel on a regular basis that you don't even notice anymore because they've become so habitual. Perhaps you walk into the kitchen and automatically open the pantry door to see if there's anything good to eat. Maybe you automatically light up a cigarette every time you take a coffee break at work. Maybe you turn on the TV as soon as you walk in your front door. Those habits have become like a tail that is wagging the dog. They are controlling you; you are not controlling them.

That's dangerous. You have to start observing yourself to see what some of those insidious habits are. I want you to identify the patterns you're holding onto that aren't serving you anymore. Any emotional state you frequently feel is a habit. Do you think of yourself as a moody person? As long as you keep thinking of yourself that way, that's what you'll be. Stop justifying being grouchy just because you feel grouchy. Feeling moody has become a habit.

It doesn't even matter what your trigger is. The dogs salivated because they heard the bell, right? I'm going to go out on a limb here, but I'd bet that if you asked them, they wouldn't have been able to tell you they were salivating because they heard the bell. It was an unconscious habit. They didn't think about it. They just did it.

Same with us. You don't have to dig into your past to figure out why you feel depressed, grouchy, or lazy. Just retrain yourself so you start feeling optimistic, upbeat and energetic. I'm going to show you exactly how to do that.

You Can Overcome Pavlovian Training

"Success is not the key to happiness. Happiness is the key to success. If you love what you are doing, you will be successful."
— *Albert Schweitzer*

The first thing you need to do is figure out which habits are pushing you away from a successful life. I'm talking here about habits of action, attitude, belief, focus and emotional states. You may think you need to hold onto those habits — just like Linus needed to hold onto that dirty blanket. You've convinced yourself that you need them for security, because they've become part of you, or whatever. But you don't need them. Let them go. Your habits don't define who you are. Your habits are simply things you did over and over. You didn't intend to train your unconscious mind to make these things a habit. The habits just accumulated.

Look at each of the four life categories we're focusing on in this program. What is your natural mindset? What's the first thing you think of when you wake up each day? How is your energy right now? What does your energy feel like when you feel ready for anything that comes at you? What are your communication habits in your relationship with your kids? With your significant other? How do you habitually treat people, your co-workers, or your boss? Start identifying the behaviors you automatically embrace that aren't serving you.

Now, instead of judging yourself or beating yourself up for doing things that don't support you, just say, "Interesting." Notice that this word doesn't judge or belittle. It simply makes you aware of what you're doing, and being aware of what needs to be changed is always the first step to change.

Believe it or not, it's not important to know why you developed the habit or where it came from. You don't have to go back and figure out why Pavlov was doing this experiment with his dogs. It doesn't matter. The only important issue is that you take the time to condition new habits. You didn't become who you are overnight, and you won't make changes overnight either. Be patient. It takes time and it takes consistent effort.

Want to know another way you can unearth all those habits you want to change? Find someone you trust completely; someone you know is absolutely looking out for your best interests. Ask that person, "What are some of the things that I'm doing on a regular basis that might be hurting me? Is there an action, habit, or predictable response that you think is keeping me from being my best self?" Ask your friends to answer those questions for each of the four categories of your life (mindset, energy, relationships, and career).

Let your friend know you want honest feedback. Reassure this individual that you're not looking for criticism. You're looking for constructive feedback so you can pinpoint what you can correct to build a happier, more successful life.

Are Those Rats Still Hanging Around?

> *"The rat had no morals, no conscience, no scruples, no consideration, no decency, no hint of rodent kindness, no compunctions, no higher feeling, no friendliness, no anything."*
>
> — *E. B. White*

I guess E. B. White didn't like rats. Well, to tell you the truth, neither do I. To me, rats are like bad habits that dirty up our life.

I had a friend in college who was something else. You couldn't give this guy any type of feedback whatsoever. If he was on his way out for a date and had something stuck in his teeth, you couldn't tell him. He took it all as criticism, as if we were picking on him just to be mean. We were just trying to help the guy. But OK, everyone has his own way of doing things. One day, a bunch of us were sitting around watching TV in a drafty old house that our friend had rented.

There we were, laughing about something on the TV, when this *big* rat ran across the room. I mean a big rat. We all jumped up and looked at our friend, who was just looking at the TV like he didn't see that huge hairy creature run across the room. Nobody said anything, because no one wanted to be the "bearer of bad tidings" and tell him he had a huge rat in his house. He was so hypersensitive, we just knew he'd take it as a personal insult.

The other guys started looking at me, making those funny, silent faces that mean, "*You* do it." So I did.

I walked over to my friend (who was still watching TV, pretending he hadn't seen a thing) and I asked, "Did you see the rat run across the room?"

He responded with the ever original come-back, "What rat?"

I said, "Either you have a really ugly Chihuahua you haven't told us about, or a rat just ran across the room."

Wouldn't you know, he looked me square in the eye and said, "Look man, if you don't want to be here, get out. And that goes for all of you."

And, that's what some people do. They take their rats personally. They are so insecure they will never, ever, admit they have any bad habits. We just asked if he saw the rat. It had nothing to do with him. It wasn't even his house. But that's what people do. They take their rats personally.

"Don't tell me about my faults!" they cry. The thing is, a response is not a fault, it's only conditioning. And that response is not even originating in the conscious mind; it's the unconscious mind ignoring those rats, also known as habits. If you have a habit that's really a rat, change it. Identify those habits that are no longer supporting you and get rid of them.

So what's the best way to do that? Would you put out a trap? The trap might catch rats one by one. But where did that rat come from? Are you sure there's only one? You will never get rid of them all until you take out the trash that's attracting them in the first place. Remember, we talked about this earlier. If you have rats in your house (bad habits), it's probably a safe bet that you have trash in your house. The rats aren't the problem. They're there to eat the trash. They're a good thing. At least somebody is trying to clean up. It's not the rats that are bad; it's the trash that's bad. We can get so busy trying to get rid of the rats that we don't even think about cleaning up the trash.

For example, some of us do that with our physical bodies. We eat anything and everything, as much as we want, whenever we want, and we end up having health problems. What do we do then? We go to the doctor and get some medicine to take care of our health problems. All the while, we keep eating and drinking everything we can get our hands on. That's a perfect example of trying to get rid of the rats and not cleaning up the trash. The rats wouldn't stick around if the environment were clean!

Remember what our trash is? Our trash is what we focus on. Our trash is what we say to ourselves on a daily basis. Our trash is our physical expression, our body language, the way that we carry ourselves. What we put in our system, that's the trash. We have to clean it up. The rats will leave when there's nothing to eat.

Smelly Emotions That are Real, but Not Unchangeable

"My friend thought he'd never get a date. I told him to think positive. Now he's positive he's never going to get a date."

— Brother Sammy Shore

Some of the most insidious habits we have are habits of attitude. That's right. Our attitudes are also habits. We've trained our emotions into our system and then, when they pop up, we make them real. It's very important to understand you don't have to "go with" whatever you're feeling just because you're feeling it.

A buddy of mine was asking me why he always ended up feeling the same way about all his intimate relationships. His problem was that whatever he felt in the moment he accepted as real and unchangeable. And he had been feeling the same emotions for twenty years. So, new people and new relationships would come into his life, and he would face them with the same smelly emotions he had been justifying for years.

Remember Pavlov's dogs salivating when they heard a bell? This man's emotional habits were like that. He would get to a certain point of the relationship and start losing interest, and he didn't even know why. He would start focusing on what was wrong with this woman and she'd lose her appeal, and he didn't even know why.

I'll tell you why: at some point in his past, to deal with a certain situation, perhaps because he was scared of commitment, he created a certain attitude. And now that situation is long gone, but the attitude turned into a habit and it is still there. He needed to break that habit if he ever wanted to develop a meaningful, long-term relationship. If he wanted a more positive dating experience, he was going to have to turn around his automatic, knee-jerk tendency to become critical.

One Way to Stop Overeating and Get What You Really Want

"To become what you are capable of becoming is the only end of life."
— *Robert Louis Stevenson*

It's all well and good to warn you to stay away from unwanted habits, but what about when you find yourself in the middle of one? Have you completely blown it? No, in fact, when you notice yourself falling into a negative habit, that's the exact right time to work on retraining yourself.

When you notice yourself going into a habitual emotion or action that is not good for you, you need to do something called a "pattern interrupt." This is a technique from Neuro Linguistic Programming (NLP). What you do with a pattern interrupt is use your physical expression to stop the pattern that you are running. You break the pattern by changing your physical expression.

Now remember, physical expression is 55% of all communication, both with yourself and with other people. That's more than half of what makes communication work, which makes changing your physical expression the fastest and most effective way to break a pattern.

When I catch myself in a pattern that's not serving me, I drastically change my physical expression in some way. What I'm doing is "scrambling" the pattern that I'm interrupting. You scramble a pattern by using your body; by getting up and drastically moving your body. Move. Move radically. Jump, skip, dance, move your body. Get as crazy as you want to with this one. I wish I could show you this physically, but I think you get it.

Here's an example: let's say that you have a pattern of overeating. The next time you notice yourself eating too much, jump out of your chair, dance around in a circle and point to yourself while shouting "Oink, oink, oink!" That will scramble your pattern of overeating. If you keep doing it and doing it and doing it, you'll soon demolish the pattern. You'll demolish the habit, even if there are some restaurants you won't be able to go back to. In the next chapter, I'll show you how to develop new habits to replace the old ones. You'll be retraining yourself to go into a better emotional state, and over time, that new emotional state will become a habit.

So, anytime you find yourself in a pattern that you don't want to indulge in, jump up and move! After you change your physical expression, you want to change your self-talk. You can even say "Stop! That's not me." You want to make sure you communicate with yourself in a way that serves you.

Finally, change what you're focusing on. The best thing to do is to concentrate on your Vision. Stop tormenting yourself with those "why" questions: "Why do I do this?" and "Why do I act this way?" You do what you do and act the way you act because you make your feelings real. Remember, your feelings aren't always real, sometimes they're just habits. Stop justifying them. The more you justify a habit, the harder it is to change. You can become what you are capable of becoming if you focus on acting instead of feeling.

Easy in the End

*"I don't wait for moods. You accomplish nothing if you do
that. Your mind must know it has got to get down to
earth."*

— *Pearl S. Buck*

As you're working on your habits, sometimes you're going to
want to quit. You know what? So what. Remember, your feelings
always follow. What I mean by that is that your feelings are a
product of your attitude habits. So when you don't "feel" like
doing something, interrupt the pattern, get your self-talk in line
and focus on what you really want. Raise your standards and then
live by them.

As I've said before, and will say again, most things that are hard
to do in the beginning are easy to live with in the end. And the
things that are easy to do in the beginning are hard to live with in
the end.

Identifying what habits need to be changed is the first step. But it's
not the only step. Just because you have consciously recognized
the habits that are not helping you doesn't mean they're going to
disappear into thin air. Remember, the job of your unconscious
mind is to keep everything the same. So if the going gets tough,
keep going. It will take ongoing effort to interrupt and turn
around those unwanted habits. However, you can accomplish it if
you put your mind to it.

Thank You, Charlie

*"I thought: 'It's now or never. Either I cling to everything
that I know, or else I develop more initiative, do things on
my own'."*

— *Agatha Christie*

I had the privilege of witnessing an amazing moment at a Tony
Robbins event with about 2,000 people. Tony called on a woman
in the audience to share her story. As she was talking, she pulled
off her wig, and we could see that she only had splotches of her
natural hair.

She said that at a very young age she had started pulling her hair out to make herself unattractive so that her father would stop molesting her. Her father had been dead for twenty years now, but her challenge was that she still couldn't sleep at night.

When she was younger it was important for her to stay awake, because if she was awake when her father came into her room, he would leave her alone. At that time, she had created in her mind a little, old black man named Charlie to play the piano all night long. Every night, Charlie would play the piano so she could stay awake.

Tony hugged her and made her feel comforted and warm, and then asked her if she would like to be able to sleep at night now. What was keeping her awake, even twenty years after her father had died, was simply a very powerful pattern that she could change.

In a loving voice, Tony asked her to close her eyes and find Charlie at his piano. She found Charlie and gave him a hug. Charlie hugged her back and told her how happy he was that she was safe now.

As Tony guided this woman through the visualization, it turned out that Charlie had a favor to ask. Charlie said that he would really like to go home and sleep. He said that he hadn't slept in 20 years because he wanted to make sure she was OK, but if she felt safe now, could he please stop playing the piano and go home. She started to cry. She thanked Charlie for all that he had done for her, gave him a kiss on the cheek and lovingly sent him home. That night, this woman slept soundly for the first time in over 20 years.

Are you clinging to something you've been doing for years? Is it time to let go of that fear, change that habit, or break that ritual? So much of our lives are patterns, and the patterns stay with us even when the outside circumstances change. What patterns are you still running in your life that you can lovingly release? Say "Thank You," and let go now.

The Seven Deceivers

"The better we feel about ourselves, the fewer times we have to knock someone down in order to feel tall."
— Odetta

You know about having a Vision and how important that is. You also know the first step towards reaching that Vision is to get rid of your old, unwanted habits. I really hope you are genuinely proud of yourself at this point because starting the journey is half the battle. You are also getting to the point where you may start struggling a little. I want to help you out before you get there, so you can make it through the tough times.

The greatest security comes from understanding how to use the principles of universal law. My son was studying the physical laws of nature in science class a little while ago. He was grumbling about having to learn about these laws because he just wasn't interested in them. I was trying to help him see that once you learn the laws that tell you how the universe works, then you can build things and create what has never before been created.

That's exactly what you're doing in this program: You're learning how your unconscious mind works so that you can use that knowledge to your advantage and create whatever you want for yourself in life.

Remember the Cycle of Performance from Chapter One? The second phase of that cycle is called Deception. That's where things start to get rough. This is when you or someone around you starts "knocking you down." If you stand your ground against these mind bullies, they will no longer have the power to knock you off your path.

There are seven main patterns people rely on during the Deception phase to feel comfortable, safe, and certain. I call these the Categories of Deception: Victim, Rut Dweller, Certainty Seeker, Success Seeker, Pretender, Escapist and Stressed Achiever. I've seen people adhere to these patterns for as little as one hour and for as long as several decades. You will unconsciously begin to exhibit these patterns when you run into difficulty. This is a normal reaction to when you hit the Deception phase. The more aware you are of what's happening, the more quickly you can move through the Deception phase and on to the Transformation phase in which the real progress starts to show up.

None of these patterns are necessarily bad; they are simply ways of dealing with challenges. We've each trained ourselves to fall back into one or more of these patterns in order to feel safe and accepted when we aren't getting the results we know we should be getting.

See if you recognize any of your individual patterns in these descriptions. Keep this in mind: These Categories of Deception are context-related, meaning that you may not be adhering to these patterns in every area of your life. You may be exhibiting one pattern of Deception in your career life, but a different one when it comes to your relationships. Be willing to put yourself on the line and look at your patterns without any judgment.

The Victim —
Some People Have to Remember to Take Responsibility

"Some people cling to pains, real and imagined, to excuse what they have become."
— *Lillian Hellman*

Someone is always taking advantage of the Victim. Somehow, he always ends up on the short end of the stick. He expects people to abuse him, or lie to him, or hurt him. If he would look objectively at his life, he would realize that this happens over and over and over again. Sometimes a Victim will think, "Maybe that's just my fate; I was born to be a victim." Many times he doesn't even realize that he has a choice in what happens to him.

The Victim sees himself perpetually at the mercy of people, circumstances and situations around him. The majority of his focus is on himself and how he is affected by the outside events, and his mood is controlled by what is happening in his world at that moment. To him, the world is a place where negative experiences are to be expected and people are not to be trusted. The

Victim has a strong need to feel certain and tends to see the world in extremes: right or wrong, black or white.

The Victim is also a master at making excuses and holding other people and events responsible for everything that goes "wrong" in his life. Because a Victim feels that everything is happening "to" him, he works desperately to gain control by attacking and using guilt tactics to achieve a sense of power over the situations and the people in his world. He will not allow people in his immediate world to choose their own experiences if this threatens his feeling of certainty. In his mind the Victim rationalizes that he is acting for the greater good.

Victims Snatch Defeat from the Jaws of Victory

"If you feel like you're a second-class citizen, you are."
— Ted Turner

Years ago, an acquaintance had a great business idea and wanted to partner with my company. He was one of the smartest men I've ever met, so I thought it was worth exploring. We set up meetings and talked a lot, and I initially thought his plan made a lot of sense. But when it came time to make the final decision, I turned him down.

Why? During all those meetings and phone calls, I had listened very closely to everything he said. What stood out to me was how often he felt taken advantage of, how his previous partners tried to rip him off, and how it was so important that he protect himself. Case after case, same theme. He even mentioned that he wanted to work with me because he knew I would treat him fairly. But I know a thing or two about the type of person who always feels that people are taking advantage of him. The question is not, "Do other people treat him fairly?" The question is, "Does he think that people are treating him fairly?" And I know that this type of person will find a way to justify that he is not being treated fairly, no matter what is happening around him.

So I told him "No." He was surprised and asked why I had chosen not to partner with him. Since he asked, I told him I felt he needed to change his thinking because he was attracting these negative situations into his life. I told him about the Four Laws of Focus: what you focus on, you find; what you focus on grows, what you focus on seems real; what you focus on, you become.

About six months later, he called to tell me he had found a wonderful business partner. Everything was going well. He said he was actually glad I had turned him down and given him that feedback. He still thought of me as a friend, and felt he was achieving a victory in his life.

Great. I was truly happy for him and hoped the change would last. Unfortunately, I got another call from him a couple of months after that. Guess what? His new partner was taking advantage of him, sabotaging information, not honoring his contract, etc.

What this individual didn't understand was he was creating everything that was showing up in his life. Let me repeat that in a more general sense: You have created most of what shows up in your life. I absolutely understand that there are exceptions-random elements of genetics, crime, disease, or lightning. Still, you create almost everything that shows up.

So, my advice to the Victim, or the person who plays that role, is to always remember this: Everything you have in your life you've attracted, you've created. So if you keep getting in those situations, it's because you're attracting those situations with your thinking. You're responsible. The only thing a Victim has to do is take responsibility. So, take responsibility.

And remember that responsibility is not about guilt, shame, or blame; responsibility literally means the "ability to respond." Realize that you've created everything that's happened, and you also have the power to create something new. You are not the same person you were yesterday, not physically and not emotionally. So, if "tragedies" have happened to you in the past, there is no reason to let those past events maintain control over you today.

Forgiveness is giving up the hope of a better past. Forgive anyone that you think may have hurt you. And most importantly, forgive yourself. You can start today to change what shows up in your future. This is not an unknown or uncertain process; it all happens according to universal laws.

The Rut Dweller — *Other People Have to Stay in the Game*

"I can't understand why people are afraid of new ideas. I'm frightened of the old ones."

— John Cage

When the Rut Dweller hits the Deception phase, he quits. The first time he hits a wall or runs into some sort of obstacle, he quits. As soon as he gets overwhelmed or frightened, he stops; he quits. He doesn't blame other people or circumstances; he just quits.

The Rut Dweller is a master of distraction. He loves to watch sports and reality TV because he gets to live vicariously through the stars; he gets to experience the life that the people on TV are living without having to risk any of the pain. He's given up on himself, and distracting himself allows him to forget about his own life.

The Rut Dweller(s) was probably a star at some point in his past (in high school, for example), and now he loves reminiscing about the "glory days" because he can see nothing in his future that could compare to those high feelings of the past.

What he can't stand, though, is that he's gaining more weight, or he's losing more money. Time is passing and things are getting worse; they're not staying the same. So the Rut Dweller finds even more ways to distract himself. He's not getting any results, and in order avoid feeling bad about himself, he lowers his standards a little bit more. The Rut Dweller won't take any time to sit down and examine his life because he doesn't want to experience that hopeless feeling.

The Rut Dweller knows that his life could be better. He looks at people who are achieving and says, "I could have done that." He'll also say things such as, "I should be out there, I should be doing this...I should, I would, I could." He never really does it; he just should, should, should. He doesn't make excuses for himself or blame others for his "failings"; he says this is just how things are and then checks the TV schedule.

My advice to the Rut Dweller is to find the courage to get back into the game of life. Put yourself out there and see what can happen. You won't know up front how things will work out, but if you keep putting those universal laws to work for you, you will succeed.

A person is either growing or dying; there really is no in-between. A Rut Dweller has to raise his standards and take small steps towards improving himself. I heard a jingle once that applies here: "Inch by inch anything's a cinch. But by the yard, it's hard." Inch by inch you can make anything happen. If you take those small steps, you can raise your standards.

You also never know if something is really going to be hard or not until you start. I remember some things I thought would be so hard to do, and I would prepare so much for them, and then I would do them and they would end up being easy tasks. I psyched myself out for nothing. I believe that, if we take the right approach, we're going to find out that life gets easier and easier because we're going to be using more of our unconscious mind. The circumstances aren't going to get easier, but we'll be able to deal with them so much more easily than before.

The Certainty Seeker —
Then There Are Those Who Need to Shake Up Their Patterns

"Progress is a good word, and change is its motivator."
— *Robert Kennedy*

The Certainty Seeker is looking for certainty above all else. Fear of change is his primary focus in life. It is important that things stay the way they are, the way they have always been. He absolutely does not want to do anything differently.

When the Certainty Seeker comes to an obstacle, he quits because he's afraid. He's not afraid of the obstacle; he's afraid of change. See, a Certainty Seeker might talk a good talk, but he really doesn't want to change because he'd rather have certainty and security than results. And, in order to get the results you want to get in this world, you have to step out on a limb and do things differently. The Certainty Seeker is not doing anything differently. He's not looking to change, expand, or progress; he just wants to stay in the comfort zone that he feels is safe. He insulates himself from the outside world by surrounding himself with other Certainty Seekers and by living in a defined environment.

Tradition is very important to him, and he has the need to belong to organized groups. He sometimes gravitates towards organized religion not for spiritual sustenance, but because religion is unchanging and the rules of the religion provide stability and certainty.

The Certainty Seeker is like the tree standing tall and strong in the face of the howling wind, the howling wind of change. He looks over at the bamboo tree bent at a 45-degree angle and is sad that the poor bamboo is going to be blown away by the wind. But the tree that is about to fall is the tree that's not bending.

That tall tree might look strong, and it might look solid, but that wind is working on that tree even more than on the bamboo. The bamboo is bending, and it's giving to the wind, but it's not breaking. It's flexible. It will bend, and it will spring back. But that mighty tree that tries to stand against the winds of change is inevitably going to break. And when it breaks, it's going to fly off and cause havoc as it tears through your house. You've seen scenes like this on the weather channel.

And that's what happens in every area of life. It's not right, and it's not wrong; it's just the way things are. What worked for you in the past may not work for you now. You have to change your strategies. Be careful about confusing tradition with principle.

The Certainty Seeker needs to understand that certainty and security come from the inside, from the ability to step out and deal with uncertainty. There is no such thing as security and certainty outside of yourself. You have to change; you either change or you die. Change is good.

The Success Seeker —
And Those Who Need to Stick with It

"When you're up to your hind end in alligators, it's hard to remember that your purpose is to drain the swamp."
— George Napper

When the Success Seeker hits the Deception phase, he stops what he's working on and looks for something new. He is convinced that there is something "out there" that will help him get the result he wants. Because he is very upbeat and positive about life, he sees this as being flexible and looking for another solution, instead of seeing it as giving up and running away.

He doesn't stop long enough to recognize that he needs to work on the internal confidence and courage that are required to take him to the next level. He is convinced that the secret to turning his life around is in the next tape program, the next book, or the next seminar. The Success Seeker doesn't get the final result that he's looking for because he doesn't stick with any one project long enough to see the results; he tends to get stuck in an endless loop of Inception–Deception– Inception–Deception– Inception–Deception. In a way, the Success Seeker is always looking for another alligator so that he doesn't have to drain the swamp.

The Success Seeker is constantly *looking* to grow and improve, and he becomes addicted to learning without necessarily growing. He goes to seminars and reads tons of books, but he doesn't take action on what he's learned. He'll say things like, "Oh, that program was great, but it didn't work for me." Or, "I've read 1,000 books, and I'm sure this new one is the one that's going to work." Or, "I'm listening to these new tapes and I just know they're really going to help me."

The flaw in the Success Seeker's game plan is that he is searching for something outside of himself to give him success. He hasn't stopped to work on his lack of confidence and courage that he needs to take himself to the next level. He hasn't really, really faced the fire yet.

So, in his own unique way, he runs. He runs because he's not ready to face the test that's going to push him through to the next level. He runs from committing to that face in the mirror that he is going to be the best that he can be. He looks for that one thing that will be more exciting, more strategic, and more positive and that will finally lead him to success.

My advice to the Success Seeker is to take action and stay focused on one thing until he sees results. The Success Seeker has to take action on all the information he has gathered. He needs to look inside himself for the answers he is seeking; all the greatness he is looking for is right there, inside himself.

He also needs to engage his emotional muscle to keep going when he hits Deception; instead of running off and looking for something new to try, he needs to make a commitment to staying with what he's doing and working through that Deception.

The Pretender — *Some People Need to Find the Love*

"A person who is nice to you, but rude to the waiter, is not a nice person."
> — *Dave Barry*

The Pretender consciously puts a mask on so that other people will see only what he wants them to see. On the outside, the Pretender looks like he has it all together, but deep down he feels insecure and emotionally unworthy. Most of the time, he won't even admit to himself how he feels. He has two identities: an internal identity and an external identity. His main fear is that he will be "found out," and that someone will discover that he really is a fraud.

When the Pretender hits Deception, he starts lying. He doesn't tell the truth. He'll do all the right things to make you think that everything is OK in his life, but he really feels as if everything is falling apart. It's hard to connect with a Pretender because of the mask he puts on for the benefit of other people.

The Pretender thinks that he has to pretend things are better than they are because, at the core, he doesn't really like himself. That's the challenge. He doesn't love himself at the core. He's looking for love and approval from some outside source, and he thinks that he can get love through what he does, what he says, how he looks. But he doesn't really feel any love inside. He doesn't really feel any love from his own heart.

A lot of celebrities fall into this category. In fact, they're driven to attain significance because they think that significance will give them the love they are not getting from themselves. The Pretender believes that if other people see him as significant and important, then he will feel worthy. Even though a Pretender may be very successful, he won't feel fulfilled inside.

He doesn't blame others for the events of his life, but he also hasn't figured out that people aren't really thinking about him in the first place. He also makes sure that his schedule is full, and he avoids time alone so that he doesn't have to look inside himself and take stock of who he's being or what he's doing.

I tell all the Pretenders that I know that the thing they need most is to love themselves. You have to really love yourself. You have to love who you are. You have to be nice to yourself and to other people. You have to appreciate yourself and be grateful for who you are. Everyone has the need and the desire to feel worthy; the Pretender has to acknowledge his own worth first.

The Escapist — *Some People Have to Face Reality*

"Reality leaves a lot to the imagination."
                                                   — John Lennon

When the Escapist hits Deception, he may go into an immediate action mode. He understands the need for change, but doesn't know what the "right" decision is, so he hides in a flurry of activity. He may also lapse into complete denial about what's really happening and generate an even stronger sense of conviction about the "correctness" of his decision.

The Escapist is a strong, persistent individual who makes a decision and then holds on to that decision, no matter what the outcome is. He is not one to evaluate the results he is getting or to change direction if those results are not meeting his original objectives.

The Escapist doesn't want to hear that he has made an unwise choice or that there may be a better way to accomplish what he is trying to do. Once he decides on a path, he will put his head down and continue until outside circumstances force him to change. Instead of listening to different viewpoints, he defends his decisions with self-righteous intensity.

Many Escapists hide from life by creating an alternate reality. They may join a cult, a militia, or a political movement and devote all their free time and energy to it. Their entire identity shifts to focus on the organization they have chosen. Their life revolves around that organization.

The Escapist doesn't notice that replacing his life with this alternate reality isn't creating the life he truly wants because he won't stop long enough to evaluate the results he is getting. If his life or plan is off course, he will go into denial and tell you that everything is going exactly the way he wants it to go.

My advice to the Escapist is to take an honest look at yourself and your life. You need to believe in yourself and know that if you've made a decision that hasn't worked out, it's not a bad reflection on you, it simply means it's time to make a different decision. My advice is that it's not too late to create the results you want by getting on a different path that takes you where you truly want to go.

The Stressed Achiever —
And Others Need to Bring the Wine to the Table

"No man (woman) who is in a hurry is quite civilized."
— Will Durant

When the Stressed Achiever hits an obstacle, he puts his head down like a bull and runs straight through it. He doesn't care who gets hurt, as long as he reaches his goal. But when he does reach his goal, he's stressed out because he doesn't get the joy he thought he would get from it, so he either looks for another goal or shuts down. That's what the Stressed Achiever does.

The Stressed Achiever is into achieving to be happy: "I won't be happy until I get this. I won't be happy until I get that. I won't be happy until I accomplish this." He goes all out and leaves it all on the table; he's almost obsessed with whatever it is he's doing, and everybody around is stressed from having to deal with him.

The challenge for the Stressed Achiever is that he's hurrying through the journey, he's not enjoying it. Any goal he reaches is a stressed achievement. He's using his willpower to knock down walls, so that some day he'll be able to relax and enjoy life. He's thinking, "Once I get this amount of money, once I get this relationship, once I get this job, I'm going to relax, I'm going to be happy." What he doesn't realize is that that's not how it works if a person wants to be truly successful. You have to be relaxed and happy as you're going about it.

My advice to the Stressed Achiever is that you have to create the meanings that allow you to enjoy every aspect of what you're doing. You have to bring that enjoyment to the table if it's not there. Sometimes you have to bring the wine. If there's no wine at the dinner table, you bring it so that you can enjoy dinner more. You have to bring the laughter, you have to bring the joy, you have to bring the harmony, you have to bring the fun; you have to bring all these things to the table.

What the Stressed Achiever has to understand is that life is about the journey not the achievement. Life is about happily achieving, not achieving to be happy. The Stressed Achiever needs to remove the stress from the achievement: keep the intensity, remove the stress. "Do" with gratitude and joy and happiness. Enjoy the process. You can keep the intensity that's great, but you must let go of the stress.

The Goal — *The Ultimate Performer*

"What saves a man is to take a step. Then another step."
— Antoine de Saint-Exupery

Ideally, we all want to be the Ultimate Performer. The Ultimate Performer has perspective about life. He realizes that life is about growing in knowledge and love and unity, and taking care of ourselves to the best of our abilities. He knows that we all need to lighten up and realize that this thing called life is the best comedy that we could ever find. The Ultimate Performer understands that we all have 86,400 seconds every day to use, and he keeps checking in with himself to make sure that he is using them wisely.

The Ultimate Performer meets the Deception phase by just continuing on a path of improving and doing it at a pace that allows him to appreciate and be grateful for what he's already accomplished. He works in little, bite size pieces that grow into habits in every area of his life, and he understands that life is about growing and getting just a little bit better every day.

If he catches himself not growing, the Ultimate Performer becomes curious about why he's hit a plateau. He doesn't beat himself up or give up; he takes an honest look at what is going on with himself and in his life. Maybe he'll see that he needs a rest right now, or maybe he'll see that there's a better way to reach his goal.

The important thing is that he keeps taking steps. He knows that, as long as he does, he'll keep growing just a little bit more every day, and all the positive actions and attitudes he is practicing will become a habit. He knows that, as these constructive actions and attitudes turn into constructive habits, his unconscious mind will imprint them and make it even easier for him to reach his goals.

It's Not Bad, It Just Is

"My parents told me I'd never amount to anything because I procrastinated too much. I told them, 'Just you wait'."
— *Judy Tenuta*

Remember, whatever patterns of Deception turn up in your life, they're just there to protect you. Change them as quickly as possible. Figure out which ones sound like you, and plan how you can do it differently the next time you encounter a challenge.

- The Victim isn't bad; he just feels the need to protect himself from the world.

- The Rut Dweller isn't bad; he just wonders if it's too late for him to change.

- The Certainty Seeker isn't bad; he just doesn't want to step out into uncertainty.

- The Success Seeker isn't bad; he's just looking outside himself for something that he already has inside.

- The Pretender isn't bad; he just doesn't like who he is and he doesn't want other people to have to be around the awful person that he thinks he is.

- The Escapist isn't bad; he just isn't able to face reality or admit that he's on a life path that isn't working.

- The Stressed Achiever isn't bad; he just thinks that the way to get significance and be happy is to accomplish his goals at all costs.

Whatever category you fall into, you're not a bad person. Like everyone else, you've just trained yourself to behave in certain ways. It's time now to choose behavioral patterns that help you instead of hurt you. First, it's time to be fearlessly honest and look at any patterns of behavior that are destructive.

Look at the patterns you're running. What do you do when you hit Deception? What do you do when the going gets tough? What are some of your tendencies? Do you have more than one Deception pattern?

Look at each of your four life categories: mindset, energy, relationship, and career. Remember, awareness of a pattern is the first step to changing that pattern.

Try This at Home —
Questions, Suggestions, and Action Plans

To Explore
- Why is it important that you break the disempowering habits in your life?
- What will you gain by getting rid of these habits?
- How will your life develop if you hang onto those disempowering habits?
- Why is it important that you free yourself from the patterns that you currently run when you are in Deception?
- What will you gain by making a shift from the Deception roles that you're currently playing to the role of Ultimate Performer?
- What will you lose if you don't make that shift?
- Where do you go in each area of your life when you hit Deception? (There can be more than one for each category, and there may be differences among categories.)

To Act

- Write down the major habits that you're committed to changing (choose at least 1 for each life category: mindset, energy, relationships and career). For example: I'm committed to changing my habit of beating myself up every time I make a mistake. I'm committed to changing my habit of overeating. I'm committed to changing my habit of complaining about my day to my spouse. I'm committed to changing my habit of spending all the money I earn every month.

- Develop a great pattern interrupt that you can use anytime you find yourself carried away by disempowering habits. Pick something outrageous that interrupts your focus, your self-talk and your physical expression. Your pattern interrupt can be anything that works for you: forcefully yelling "Stop!", standing on your head and laughing, singing and dancing to the song in your head...the possibilities are endless.

- Use your new pattern interrupt as many times as possible to interrupt old habits.

- Keep track of how often you use your pattern interrupt. Is the frequency decreasing over time?

To Remember

- Your habits feel more real than they are.

- Any habit can be changed.

- The role that you play when you're in Deception is not who you are, it is only a role that you are playing in the moment. You can change it at any time.

NOTES

In any contest between power and patience, bet on patience.

— W.B. Prescott

NOTES

You can tell more about a person by what he says about others than you can by what others say about him.

— Leo Aikman

Build New Habits

Genius is the ability to put into effect

what is in your mind.

— F. Scott Fitzgerald

Are Your Habits Helping You or Hurting You?

"Great thoughts reduced to practice become great acts."
— *William Hazlitt*

The secret to creating lasting change is to create powerful habits. Why? Well, since you're going to have habits anyway, they might as well be effective and powerful.

We are creatures of habit. We have so much to do and remember every day that if we didn't turn most of what we do into habits, we wouldn't be able to function. They have to be there. We have habits of attitudes, habits of emotions, habits of belief, habits of focus, habits of self-talk, habits of physical expression...we have habits in every area of our lives.

This section of the book shows you how to develop the habits, attitudes, beliefs, and physical expressions that are going to support you. You are going to educate yourself about which patterns of behavior are undermining you and take steps to turn them around. In the beginning, there will be a lot of uncertainty as you do things differently. But trust me that over time, you will become more comfortable with your new habits and they will benefit you for the rest of your life.

Grandma's Secret Recipe for Habits

"Recipes don't make cookies."
— *saying on a coffee mug*

I know you're excited to get going on all this, and I'm going to make it even easier on you. I'm going to give you the secret recipe for cooking up a habit.

Before I reveal the recipe, though, I need to make a very important point. I've noticed that when people start to identify their ineffective habits, they tend to get very judgmental with themselves. If you're looking for what's "wrong," you could end up getting down on yourself. That won't help the process.

Remember the distinction between your conscious and unconscious mind. I told you how I call my conscious mind by my first name and my unconscious mind by my middle name so that I can keep them separate. If something in your life is a habit, it's being controlled by your unconscious mind, and your unconscious mind doesn't evaluate good or bad, right or wrong.

Think back to those dogs that bark and bite because that's what they've been trained to do. They don't think of barking and biting as bad; they just do what they were trained to do. Your unconscious mind operates the same way. It's just doing what it's been trained to do. So, instead of giving yourself grief, give yourself credit for being willing to change.

Now for the recipe. Recipes list ingredients so you know what goes into something. If you want this something to happen, you must ACT on these ingredients.

The three ingredients of a habit are:

1. Focus.

2. Self-talk.

3. Physical expression.

Habit Ingredient #1 Is Focus: *Are You Half-full or Half-empty?*

"If it weren't for the optimist, the pessimist would never know how happy he isn't."
— message on a t-shirt

What are your habits of focus? Do you see the glass as half-full or half-empty? It's not that optimism is "good" or pessimism is "bad." The question is, which focus gets you closer to your ideal life Vision?

Maybe in your past, being a pessimist seemed to be useful. Maybe it brought you a feeling of stability or kept you from being disappointed. But focusing on what is not working in your life will only bring more of what is not working into your life (remember the

Law of Attraction?). Part of The 45 Day Challenge® is choosing to cultivate the habit of an optimistic attitude.

What do you focus on in each of the four life categories: mindset, energy, relationship, and career? Do you think about everything that is going wrong in your day, or do you call to mind everything you're grateful for? Do you focus on the things you love about the people in your life, or do you let small things annoy you? What are you choosing to focus on? That's right. What you focus on, what you think about, can be a conscious choice starting now.

Habit Ingredient #2 Is Self-Talk:
Get the Right Answer When You Talk to Yourself

"We act as though comfort and luxury were the chief requirements of life, when all we need to make us really happy is something to be enthusiastic about."
— *Charles Kingsley*

What do you say when you're alone with yourself? Yes, I'm talking about those under-your-breath ramblings, but I'm also referring to what you're saying to yourself inside your head, for no one to hear but you. What is your dialogue with yourself? Is it enthusiastic? Is it depressing? Does it build you up or bring you down? What questions do you ask yourself consistently? Are they "why" questions? "Why am I so screwed up?", "Why does this always happen to me?" and "Why did I blow it again?"

The quality of the answer that you get depends on the quality of the question that you ask. What are your self-talk habits? Think about those universal laws I told you about. Your self-talk is the primary way you direct your focus. What you focus on, you will attract into your life. You — and only you — are in control of what you focus on and what you say to yourself. I once heard a former prisoner-of-war speak to a group. After he had finished, my friend commented, "I know that was a terrible ordeal, but he used his mind to give him better days in prison than I was sometimes giving myself in my comfortable life at home."

Most of your habitual self-talk is unconscious; you're not even aware of the dialogue that goes on between your conscious and unconscious minds. What I'm asking you to do here is consciously choose what your "Erving" hears and therefore acts on. Choose phrases that will benefit you, and then repeat them consistently with as much intensity and emotion as you can muster. These phrases repeated over and over with intense emotion are your incantations.

When you created your Vision, you were careful to state all your desires in the positive, right? The same "must" applies to your self-talk. If you want to quit smoking, you don't say to yourself, "I don't want to smoke, I don't want to smoke, I don't want to smoke." From that message, your unconscious mind will hear, "smoke, smoke, smoke."

What you want to say instead would be something like, "I am healthy, I am healthy." "I am" is a very powerful phrase because one of the strongest forces in human nature is the need for your unconscious mind to hold tight to the identity that you hold for yourself. When you attach the words "I am" to a thought, you are telling your unconscious mind that this is the identity that you hold for yourself. So if you're saying to yourself, "I am a loser," that is very, very, very powerful language and it's going to have an impact on your habits and your sense of self-worth.

What are you attaching "I am" to? I have clients that tell me they use negative "I am" statements to motivate themselves consciously. I am speaking truth when I say that those statements are sending a clear-cut message to your unconscious mind, and your unconscious mind will act on them.

The unconscious mind has a lot more power than the conscious mind. It has access to resources that the conscious mind has not even dreamed of.

So, if you have to choose between satisfying your conscious mind and satisfying your unconscious mind, you have to do what's best for your unconscious mind, no question about it. You have to get rid of the "I am" with the negatives behind it.

The key here is to separate the behavior from the person. You can be critical of your behavior and say things like, "I'm acting stupid." That is very different from saying, "I am stupid." Can you see the difference? When you say, "I'm acting..." you are judging your actions in the moment, not who you are universally.

However, when you say "I am..." you are making a statement about who you are, and that defines what your unconscious mind holds as your identity. I sometimes say to myself, "I'm behaving inconsistently with who I really am." That motivates me consciously and unconsciously, and helps me support a positive, optimistic attitude that moves me towards my Vision more powerfully.

This same principle applies to talking to other people, especially children. You have to be very careful when communicating to your kids. Don't say, "You are bad." You can say, "You're acting badly, and that's not who you are," but never label them negatively as a person. Never define anyone, including yourself, with a negative label. Everyone has the ability to change and grow and become even better than who they are now, but if those negative labels become their identity, change and growth become very difficult.

Habit Ingredient #3 Is Physical Expression: *Your Golf Game Can Improve Your Life*

"If you don't take care of your body, where will you live?"
— sign in gym

Did you know that how you use your face and body can determine how you feel? Your biochemistry, which is controlled by what you put into your body (e.g., food, drugs, alcohol, cigarette smoke), also determines whether you are pumped up or down in the dumps.

Have you ever watched Tiger Woods after he makes a phenomenal golf shot? Have you seen him pump his arm with that intense look on his face? Have you ever seen his stride as he walks up the fairway to hit his next shot? Whether his last shot was good or bad, the structure of his body language is the same: confident, composed and kingly. He's pouring in that third ingredient, his physical expression of what he wants to happen and who he wants to be. He doesn't always play his "A" game. But he approaches every shot as if it were an "A" shot. When you stand strong, you feel strong.

The trick is that your body guides your emotions. That's right. If you want to feel happy, act happy with your body. That means that you should smile, hold your head up, throw your shoulders back, and put a spring in your step. If you want to feel sad, do just the opposite: frown and look down at the ground with your shoulders all slumped over and your feet dragging with each step.

Take a minute now to evaluate yourself. How do you stand? How do you move? Where are your shoulders? Are they back or stooped? How do you hold your arms, your legs, and your head? Your physical expression has everything to do with how you communicate with other people and what you communicate to yourself. What is your body saying? Do you stand strong, or are you in the habit of slumping over? Look at your habits and forget about how you acquired them. Just take a look at them where they are right now. Realize this is not about good or bad. I keep going back to that because that is an important distinction. Do you make it a habit to judge yourself and other people? If so, that is definitely a habit you need to eliminate right now. Evaluate yourself, realizing that your answers are neither good nor bad. The absence of judging yourself and others is a powerful habit that will serve you in all you do. Instead of judging, teach yourself to observe and learn.

You want your physical expression to communicate to the world that you are confident and courageous and that you belong here. Some people have no idea that their posture and their movement are that of a Victim, or a Rut Dweller. Some people carry themselves like the Rut Dweller: they walk as if they're in a rut. They dress as if they're in a rut. Some people carry themselves as if they're the Victim: they look as if they're angry at the world, and they walk looking down at the ground, slumped over as if they have nothing to be thankful for.

Carry yourself with the strength and courage of the Ultimate Performer. The more you carry yourself in that manner, the more power your physical expression adds to your incantations. Emotion is created by motion, and when you move your body in time with your incantations, you are adding the power of emotion to what you are saying. This is a very powerful tool. When you put focus and emotion together, you're going to create. In the military we used this process of adding motion to incantations to develop an identity that could turn a young person who had never before left his hometown into a young person willing to make great sacrifices for his country.

Every habit in your life, such as smoking, overeating, and laziness, is preceded by an attitude. The mistake people make is in trying to break the physical habit without breaking the attitude habit first. The reason that I've had so much success helping my clients to change their habits is because I get them to break the attitude habit before they break the physical habit.

Focus, self-talk and physical expression: those are the three ingredients that you are going to mix together to build your new habits. Your habits will get the results for you. All you need to focus on in life is building the right habits. Evaluate your habits, and recondition the ones that don't serve you. You do this by focusing on thoughts that feed your Vision, by making sure your self-talk is positive, and by holding your body tall and strong.

Have Your Cake and Eat It Too

"Nothing is a waste of time if you use the experience wisely."

— *August Rodin*

Let me put this in perspective for you: things that are hard to do in the beginning are easy to live with in the end. I know I've said that before, but I want you to really get it. Yes, you are going to have to work at creating new habits, and it's going to be hard at times. But you have to remember that the hard part will eventually be over and then the unconscious mind will be reconditioned to help you, and from then on the new habits will be easy. You will reap the rewards of your hard work from that point on.

The other side of that coin is that the things that are easy to do in the beginning are hard to live with in the end. This is my constant message to my children. Things such as doing nothing, or watching too much TV, or eating junk food, or procrastinating, or not following through: those things are easy to do right off the bat. And then they become habits and make your life harder and harder; they make it harder to get ahead, harder to get results and harder to grow. You are not going to get what you want in life if you follow these patterns of behavior.

Here's what you need to understand: Life is about being persistent. Anything that you persist in doing will become easy to do. That's what people don't understand. When something is hard to do, that just means your unconscious mind hasn't accepted it yet. So what do you do? You persist. You persist in pouring in those three ingredients of a habit, and you do it deliberately so that you make sure your ingredients support and serve you and your goals. And you know that one day, very soon, your unconscious mind is going to say, "Cool, if that's what you want, I'll make sure it keeps happening. Piece of cake. I just had to make sure you really wanted it."

Take investing as an example. When you first start investing, it's hard to do. You can think of so many other things you want to do with that money. It would feel so good right then to take that vacation or buy that new car. And then you have a choice. Do you choose what's easy to do at the moment, or what's hard to do at the moment?

If you choose what's hard to do, and invest that money no matter what, then one day you'll wake up and realize that you have accumulated wealth, more than you could have ever dreamed of. And now you can support your entire life at a higher level. You feel great about yourself and your intelligent choices, and you keep investing and expanding your wealth even more. Why? Because now it's a habit, and it's easy to do. It's part of who are, your identity, and it's very easy to live with. And now you're able to take time to help society, and you're contributing and making a difference in the world. It's just who you are.

But if you give in to temptation and choose to spend that money instead of investing it, then you'll wake up one morning and realize that you have nothing more than what you had before. Your life situation hasn't improved; you have no resources to contribute. I know that isn't a place you want to be. So, just remember these things.

When you look at your life and you look at the things that you do day-to-day, start asking yourself, "What am I doing? Is this easy to do?" And if it's easy to do, ask yourself, "Is this going to be easy to live with or hard to live with in the end?" Remember, things that are worth doing are worth the effort of pushing yourself through the hard part.

Life is about challenging yourself. If you tackle things that are hard to do right now, such as getting up earlier in the morning to go for that walk, then before you know it, one day you'll wake up and feel fitter and more vital, and you'll feel better about the way that you look.

And if, one morning, you do roll over and go back to sleep instead of getting up early and practicing your positive new habits, don't abandon your intentions and lecture yourself. Just use that experience wisely and recommit to doing what is good for you instead of what is tempting.

Pet the Dog When You Get Home

"Once a human being has arrived on this earth, communication is the largest single factor determining what kinds of relationships he makes with others and what happens to him."

— *Virginia Satir*

Did you realize that the way in which you communicate is also a habit? Your communication starts with the emotional state that you are in, your attitude. Your physical expression reflects your emotional state, and 55% of communication is non-verbal/physical expression. Fifty-five percent. That's more than half. Are you seeing how important that is? Communication is not about your words only. In fact, words count for only 7% of effective emotional communication. The other 38% of communication is carried by the tone of your voice. The thing is that most of the emotional states, or attitudes, that you live in are habitual.

I've seen this happen a lot: you have a string of bad days at work and you come home in a bad mood. The bad days pile up and you keep coming home in a bad mood. Pretty soon that bad mood is a habit. You get home and you kick the dog because you're in a bad mood. Now, one day, you have a great day at work, but when you get home, you kick the dog. You wanted to pet the dog, but as soon as you walked in the door, the bad mood came back. Why? The bad mood came back because now it's a habit, and the trigger for the habit could be as simple as driving up the driveway or walking in the front door carrying a briefcase.

It's not just the dog, though, is it? Our children are waiting to see how we act when we get home. Our habits are patterns that our children watch and learn from. Our habits are teaching our children how to act. We all have to create habits that support the kind of person we want to be and that support the kind of person we want our children to become. Remember that 55% of your communication is your body language, that your body reflects your attitude, and that your attitudes are habitual. Ask yourself, "How do I want to communicate? What attitudes or emotions are going to be great to have all the time?" Then make those attitudes a habit.

One of the biggest keys in being successful in all areas of your life is to get addicted to the process. Get addicted to the process of learning and growing. Get addicted to the process of improving and practicing. Go home and practice being great; practice with your spouse, practice with your kids. And as you are practicing, you'll start seeing the results. You'll get what you want. But don't do it so you can check it off on your to-do list; do it because you enjoy the journey. Do it because you enjoy the process. That process is part of you. The key is to make it part of your identity.

Get Ready for Opening Night

"Success often comes to those who dare and act; it seldom goes to the timid who are ever afraid of consequences."
— *Jawaharlal Nehru*

When I was in college, I signed up for acting and the drama club. We would memorize our lines and then run through the play, scene by scene. We would rehearse every day for months before the big show. Even when we thought we had it down perfectly, our acting teacher would make us continue to run through the entire play. He told us there was always another level to be reached.

That's what the principles in this book are about: creating the habits that are consistent with the ultimate Vision that you hold for your life. So now, when you want to create a new habit, you get your three ingredients together: your focus, your self-talk, and your physical expression. You practice them over and over again. You do them as if you're in a play. You rehearse. You do them over and over.

In the previous chapter, I told you about the Categories of Deception: the Victim, the Rut Dweller, the Certainty Seeker, the Success Seeker, the Pretender, the Escapist, and the Stressed Achiever. The patterns that these categories represent become habits because you do them over and over and over. The way to create new, more successful patterns is not to wallow in doubt and tell yourself all the reasons it won't work; it's to start acting the way you want to, over and over and over.

What you ultimately want in life is to be that Ultimate Performer. You want this to be automatic, and the way you make it automatic is to practice, practice and practice again, and to be fully associated while you do it. That means you put your entire heart and soul into everything you do. Do it over and over and over again.

My Granddad told me, "Make sure everything you do is important to you. If you do that, you'll be successful." When people are trying to lose weight I always tell them the same thing: you didn't put the weight on in a day, don't expect to take it off in a day. Same with smoking: you didn't start with a two pack a day habit, don't expect to quit in one day, either. Just persist, stick to your new actions and attitudes. Remember, what's hard in the beginning ends up being easy as you progress through it.

Why Not Do Your Own 100 Push-Ups?

"I ran and ran and ran every day, and I acquired this sense of determination, this sense of spirit that I would never, never give up, no matter what else happened."
— Wilma Rudolph

One day my wife decided that she wanted to be able to do 100 push-ups. She asked if I could help her develop this as a habit. She said that she could already do 30.

Great. I told her I had a plan. "For the next 7 days," I said, "do 10 push-ups each day."

She wanted to do 30, but I told her that if she really wanted to get to 100 push-ups, she would be better off focusing on the process rather than on instant achievement. I encouraged her to start as a learner and follow a plan. I explained that determination is important, but that it must be coupled with a smart plan so that we're setting ourselves up for success.

For that first week, she did 10 push-ups every day of the week and complained that it wasn't even a good work out. Fine.

The second week, I asked her to do 20 push-ups each day. Her body was changing, but it still wasn't a stretch for her yet. The third week, the plan called for 30 push-ups, which was her max before. Now, even 30 push-ups wasn't even a stretch. After 30, she added 5 push-ups each week to her daily total.

Pretty soon, it became a habit for her to do push-ups every morning. Her whole nervous system, blood flow, all her muscles, every part of her body wanted to do push-ups every morning. She said it was just like brushing her teeth. She just did it every morning. So, every week my wife increased the number of push-ups by 5. Right on schedule, she was at 100 push-ups.

When you train your unconscious mind to do the right things, it will. Just as it works against you when you are starting to make a change, it will work for you once you repeat your new action enough times; it will urge you to do things that it has been conditioned to do.

Now in the beginning, there were days when my wife didn't even want to do her 10 push-ups, but because she knew 10 would be so easy, she did them anyway. Over time, doing push-ups became a habit. The plan set her up to win. Because I knew it would be hard mentally for her to get herself to actually do the push-ups, I created the plan to make the process physically easy. That plan let her build gradually on success. Remember, take action to develop a habit and then let your habits get the results for you. That way there isn't any pain for the subjective (unconscious) mind. Set yourself up to win.

Here's another really important distinction: Don't allow any exception until the new habit is firmly in place. Please mark that sentence in your mind: Don't allow any exception until the new habit is firmly in place.

What happens when you think, "Well, I can skip just one day."? You're making it hard on yourself; you're not setting yourself up to win. This is why it's important to take small enough steps in order to remain consistent. Remember, you're not trying to achieve a short-term result; you're allowing your new habit to grow so that it will one day run the show for you. Commitment and consistency are the absolute keys to creating a habit. Don't allow any exception until the new habit is firmly in place.

Keep the Sun in Your Day

"One of my main goals on the planet is to encourage
people to empower themselves."
— *Oprah Winfrey*

How do you know which habits and patterns to start creating? The first thing to do is look at your Vision. Write down the kind of person you would have to be in order to feed that Vision. What attitudes would you have to have? What would you need to believe? What actions would you need to take every day? What goals would you need to reach? How could you empower yourself?

Keep in mind that your Vision is to your life as the Sun is to the Earth. You want to make sure you focus on what will support your new Vision because you understand the four-part Law of Focus: what you focus on, you find, what you focus on grows, what you focus on seems real, and what you focus on, you become. You want to make sure you are focused on the right things consistently. You want to make sure that your self-talk, the questions you ask yourself, and how you carry your body are all in line with your Vision.

You need to realize that you are conditioning yourself at all times. That means your consistent performance is based on the attitudes you carry around all the time. Understand that. What will get you to your Vision are the day-to-day actions that you take. So many people get caught up in the big picture of the Vision that they don't place enough importance on the actions. Yes, the Vision is the CEO, and the goals are the manager, but it takes the workers (the actions) to make the company successful.

When I develop new habits, I commit to the world. I let everyone know that this is what I want to do. I let everyone know this is my new habit. And I do that because I want to stay committed to that habit. The next thing I do is take immediate action because I want to start the process rolling. I know that my old patterns are still there, but I also know how to interrupt them, and I've already made an agreement with myself that I will not beat myself up. I keep my eyes on my Vision because I know that this new habit is going to take me to that Vision, and I know that my Vision is like the sun, sustaining life. As long as you make it a habit to focus on your Vision, it will support you in developing all your other new habits.

Want to Try a $15 Million Experiment?

"In influencing others, example is not the main thing. It is the only thing."

— Albert Schweitzer

Imagine that you are being offered an opportunity to make $15 million, tax-free, without doing anything illegal or immoral. The job will take you 6 months to complete. Welcome aboard.

Here's the background: A group of wise, loving, smart, kind, strong, people were recently brought together to work on shaping a better world. These people are geniuses in every area of life: mentally, emotionally and physically.

Unfortunately, their secluded compound was hit by the fallout from a violent meteor storm. Physically they're all safe, but mentally and emotionally they are now the equivalent of newborn babies. These exceptional people have forgotten all their mental and emotional conditioning. Now, they have to relearn life; they have to relearn how to function.

Right now the group is sequestered in a holding facility. They have had no contact with the outside world. Here's what's going to happen: you are going to go meet these people and help them to learn everything they need to learn to reshape the world into a more peaceful, productive home for all its inhabitants. You will be assigned as the mentor for one of these people. You will take this person home with you and be responsible for training him for the next six months.

This won't be book-learning, though. You are going to train the person you are assigned to mentor by allowing him to follow your example. Twenty-four hours a day, he is going to be with you and mimic everything you do. That is how this person will learn to function in the world.

He can pick up on your emotions, your thoughts, everything. Everything that you do, he'll do. Everything that you need for your task will be provided for you. If you need to move to a bigger house, we'll buy you a bigger house, it doesn't matter; whatever you need. So that's your assignment. After six months, you collect your $15 million and know that you're a hero.

Now, let me ask you a question: What would you do differently knowing that your every word, your every move, is influencing the way this other person chooses to speak and act? What would you do the same and what would you change? How would you greet the day? Would you drag yourself out of bed, or jump up with energy? Would you grouse and gripe about petty problems, or would you look around with wonder and gratitude?

What would you say to yourself when you looked in the mirror? Would you call yourself a fat pig, or would you tell yourself how appreciative you are of having a body that walks, see, hears, breathes, and feels?

What would you do if you knew that this person was watching you intently? How would you act as you were driving to work? Would you curse the traffic? Would you listen to shock jocks spew verbal garbage, or would you fill your ears and mind with time-less classical melodies? What would you think about, knowing that your trainee could pick up on your thoughts?

How would you act, knowing that this pair of attentive eyes was watching your every move and learning from it? Would you goof off at work? Would you follow through on your ideas? Would you do your best? Would you step up to the next level? How would you treat your co-workers and your subordinates, or your super-visors and your leaders? Would you act with honor, with respect, and with character?

How would you act in your relationships? How would you be with your significant other, or your friends? How would you carry yourself around your kids, your parents, your brothers and sisters and cousins, or the rest of your family? How would you treat people in your community? Would you be genuine? Would you be real and would you put your energy and focus where you need to put it? Would you tell people that you love them, even if you haven't said it in a while? Would you make yourself vulnerable, knowing that vulnerability is power?

What would you do about your health and energy? Would you take care of yourself? Would you finally get up and start working out? Would you drink more water? Would you eat more vegeta-bles? Would you study what you need to know and how you need to be in order to have a happy, functional, fulfilling life? What would you do differently?

In your mind, what would you say to yourself? Would you be grateful for your life? Could you possibly muster the words "I love me"? Could you really appreciate who you are, or would you continue to focus on what you're not doing so well? What would you do differently?

And then, as you think about the things that you would do differ-ently, I want you to realize that the person watching you and learning from you...is you. You've always been there. You've always been that person with your own genius and abundant potential. What separates people who do great things with their lives from people who do horrible things are their choices. How do you choose to condition that genius that is already inside you?

It all comes down to loving who you are and realizing that you are more than a bundle of patterns that have been conditioned by other people in your life and by society. You're designed for success. You're designed for more. You're designed to grow. If you ever have to remind yourself that that person is watching, look in the mirror.

Every time you have to remind yourself to step up to the next level, pull out a mirror. Look in that mirror and resolve to change your attitude, your communication, and your actions. Look at those eyes in the mirror. You'll notice they belong to that genius part of you that wants to live life at the highest level; the part of you that longs to blossom and to grow. Look in that mirror and love who you are even more. Be grateful for who you are, and realize that people will follow your example, and that the most powerful way of giving to the world is giving through your example.

Get up from Where You Are

"There are some people who want to get rid of their past, who if they could, would begin all over again . . . but you must learn that the only way to get rid of your past is to get a future out of it."

— *Phillip Brooks*

I know that I need to do things over and over again, physically and in my mind, to make them become habits. And I know that the moment I get off track, I'll get back on. I don't cry, beat myself up, and wail that I have to start over from the beginning. I just get up from where I am and move on. I know that it's not that I'm bad, it's just that my unconscious mind is doing what it's been conditioned to do, so I forgive myself with the proper self-talk.

I am constantly forgiving myself. Constantly. As soon as we do that, we stop dwelling on the past and start building our future.

So I am constantly forgiving others and I am constantly forgiving myself because I have to move forward. Because I know that I am a co-creator, I know that I don't have time to hold anything in my mind that I don't want to create. Would you put anything in the oven that you didn't want to cook? No. So think about what is in your oven. What's in your oven is what you are holding in your focus. Be very careful about what you cook, because you have to eat what you cook, and some things aren't good to eat.

I was watching a talk show the other day. The guest was a woman who had been sober for 300 days and was depressed because she had a few beers the night before and got drunk. The host put a sad look on his face and sympathized, "Oh, I'm so sorry for you. All that time gone; now you have to start all over."

Someone needs to set that man straight. Three hundred days gone? No. What about three hundred days versus one? She was clean and sober for three hundred days and slipped up for one. She doesn't have to start over. She can start right now on 301 clean and sober days. And tomorrow will be 302 clean and sober days. She can get up and get going from where she is.

There will be moments when you mess up and want to quit. Life is not a school where they penalize you for making mistakes. How can you grow without making mistakes? How could a baby walk without falling? Should we give him an F because he fell five times and the other kid only fell four times? That doesn't make any sense.

This program is about growing and re-conditioning the unconscious mind, not about beating yourself up because you slipped. The unconscious mind is just doing its job. Remember the story about the dogs that were trained to bark and bite? Be careful about kicking your dogs. And remember that quitting can be the same as kicking your dogs. Be careful about that. Stay strong. Even if you have to pick yourself up again and again. Don't get caught up in trying to be perfect. This is not about perfect; this is about growth.

Try This at Home —
Questions, Suggestions, and Action Plans

To Explore

- Why is it important that you create new habits that empower you?
- What will your new habits give you in your life?
- What will you lose in your life if you don't create new habits?
- What will you have to focus on to build these new habits?
- What would your self-talk have to be?
- What would your physical expression look like?

To Act

- Create new habits to replace the old habits you are committed to breaking.
- Instead of beating yourself up every time you make a mistake, from now on only spend time every night listing everything you did during the day that you are proud of.

To Remember

- Consistency is the name of the game.
- Take small steps that you can sustain long-term.
- What is hard to do in the beginning is easy to live with in the end.
- Expect to work at this.
- You are given 86,400 seconds every day. Invest them wisely. There is nothing more important than your seconds.

NOTES

Dig the well before you are thirsty.

— Chinese Proverb

Discipline Your Imagination

I dream my painting,

and then I paint my dream.

— Vincent Van Gogh

CHAPTER 4

Why Not Think Like Einstein?

"Imagination is more important than knowledge."
— Albert Einstein

Imagination is where all creation happens, and that is what makes it so powerful. There is a certain way, however, to use your imagination so it adds to your life. If you don't use your imagination in this specific way, you will create things in your life that you don't want. An undisciplined imagination does whatever it wants to do. You're not consciously thinking, "Right now I'm going to focus on negative things." Your imagination is going there because it's easy, and now, it has become a habit.

You can also use your imagination to help yourself stay focused in your daily activities. Let's say that you sit down to complete a task and five minutes later you get up and do something else; you just don't feel like finishing what you were doing. That simply means you haven't disciplined your imagination, you haven't learned how to control your focus.

How to Live with Three Sisters

"I have a photographic memory, I just haven't developed it yet."
— Jonathan Winters

I like to use a parable to illustrate the difference between imagination, focus, and memory.

Imagine that you live next to a family in which there were three sisters. Each one is very different. You don't know them very well, so you make up names for each of them. The oldest sister is very conservative. She is also scared and nervous about everything; she wants to do exactly what she saw her mother and grandmother do-get married and raise a family. You decide to name this sister Memory.

The middle sister is very studious. She works hard and always gets things done. You decide to name this sister Focus.

The youngest sister has all the fun. She is talented and beautiful and everything is effortless for her. You name her Imagination.

Imagination is always excited about something. She has lots of fun and gets into lots of trouble, but she never gets anything done. She never has any sustainable results in spite of her great talent.

Focus really makes something of herself. She is very dependable and she has a career, but she never seems excited about anything.

Memory turns out just like her mother and grandmother. She gets married and lives out her life doing things the way they've always been done. She feels safe.

Guess what? We all have those three sisters living in our mind, and one of them is always running the show. Memory and Focus each know what they want, but Imagination is the most powerful sister. Memory and Focus are always fighting over Imagination, and because Imagination just wants to have fun, she doesn't care who she spends her time with.

When Memory is in charge, she uses Imagination to dwell on the past: pain, humiliation and all the reasons why those new things you tried didn't work out. Memory wants everything to stay safe and comfortable. When Focus is running the show, she uses Imagination to pull her forward towards her dreams and goals. Focus wants to take life to the next level. In the cases where Imagination breaks out on her own, she tends toward an undisciplined life: fun and exciting, but no forward results.

Since imagination is a tool that can be used either by memory or by focus, it comes down to a choice that each one of us makes. If we don't make a choice, memory steps in. That's where our habits live, in memory. When you live in memory, you end up with your future looking just like your past. The same things happen to you over and over and over. If you choose to live in focus, you need to take the next step of disciplining your imagination. If your imagination is not disciplined, your focus doesn't have any power. When you focus on your Vision and discipline your imagination, you become a mega-star. You're not just successful, you're outrageously successful. We all have access to future possibility through our imagination. Memory does not create. Only imagination creates. Imagination. Use it to create the future you want for yourself.

Win Your Dreams and Dream Your Wins

"Become so wrapped in something, you forget to be afraid."

— *Lady Bird Johnson*

Have you ever awakened from a dream with your heart beating out of control? Sometimes your dream seems so real that your emotions are engaged even though nothing has happened. The reason it seems so real is that your unconscious mind cannot tell the difference between something that is vividly imagined and something that has actually happened.

So, as far as your unconscious mind is concerned, vividly imagining something is the same as actually doing it physically. Here's the beautiful part of it: if your focus learns how to discipline your imagination, what you vividly imagine becomes a part of your memory. Because your identity is stored in memory, your whole identity begins to change. Beautiful. Also, once your memory is full of these bright, positive references, it can add to the direction of your focus instead of taking away from it.

Many studies have been done to prove this principle. I like the one with the twelve college basketball players. The scientists running the study recorded how many free-throw shots each of the twelve players could make in a given amount of time. Next, they randomly separated the players into three groups of four players each to do a one-week experiment. The first group was told to not practice: no basketball at all. The second group was told to practice free-throw shooting for one hour each day. The third group was told to imagine themselves shooting perfect free-throw shots for one hour each day, without stepping foot on a basketball court.

At the end of one week, the players got back together to shoot free-throws for the scientists. The group that did not practice showed 0% improvement. The group that physically practiced shooting baskets for one hour each day showed a 25% improvement. The group that imagined practicing for one hour each day showed a 24% improvement. Amazing. A 24% improvement using the power of imagination because their minds could not tell the difference between something that is vividly imagined and something that has actually happened.

Have you ever seen people worry about something they think is going to happen? They'll get pale and start to shake and sweat...yet nothing has happened yet. That's imagination. They are doing such a good job of creating that negative scenario in their mind that their body responds as if it's actually happening. They're worrying about things that haven't happened. That's a misuse of imagination.

If you don't consciously use your imagination, it will use you. You want to deliberately use your imagination to create vivid images of the things you want to have in life. You want to see yourself taking the actions that are going to support you. You want to wrap yourself up in what you want so you forget to be afraid.

Ride the Roller Coaster and Live Your Vision

"Strength is a matter of the made-up mind."
— John Beecher

Now you're convinced that the mind cannot tell the difference between something that it vividly imagines and something that has actually happened. When you are vividly imagining something, you are "visualizing." Visualizing is a technique used by almost every superstar athlete. It's just seeing something happen the way that you want it to happen, before it happens. Simple.

The key to visualizing is making your images big, bright, and bold; create a picture that you can see, hear, feel, taste and smell. The most effective image captures and engages all your senses. Give your image movement and energy; don't just watch yourself taking action, but put yourself in the experience; feel it.

There are no limitations on imagination. Physically we all have limitations, but in our imagination we are boundless. Use your imagination. You will get what you create in your mind. Every great leader, every great business person, every great athlete will tell you that everything starts with a Vision. It sounds so fluffy, and maybe you're sick of hearing it, but it's so true. And these are the mechanics that will bring that Vision to life.

Try this: Close your eyes and picture yourself watching a roller coaster ride. Got it? OK. Now, close your eyes and watch that same roller coaster ride, but this time instead of watching it from the ground, you're hanging on for dear life in the front car. Which image seemed more alive to you?

The image that has you in the roller coaster, instead of just watching it, gives you a much more powerful experience of riding a roller coaster. That is exactly how you want to visualize yourself living the life of your dreams. See yourself in your future life. In fact, here's one more essential key: See yourself living that life of your dreams as if it already exists. In your mind, you have already received what you are visualizing.

Consider this: When you're driving home, you have the comfort level of knowing that your house is going to be exactly where you left it this morning, right? You don't drive home every day with your stomach tied in knots saying, "I wonder if my house is going to be there today." You don't do that. You have a level of expectation. You know that when you turn that corner your house is going to be there.

That is the attitude you need to take into your visualization. Expect that what you're visualizing is going to happen. Of course it is. Make your visualization as clear in your mind as your house standing on your lawn. Wanting something is not the same as working to make it happen. Everyone wants to be happy. Everyone wants to have a great relationship, and everyone wants more money. But very few people sit down and take the time to visualize that experience already happening. Once you make up your mind that THIS is what you want, once you picture it clearly and vividly over and over, you generate the courage to take the steps to make it happen.

Enjoy Your New Car

"I've had a wonderful life. I only wish I'd realized it sooner."

— Collete

I have a grumpy neighbor who is always walking around frowning with those little creases between his eyebrows. He brought home a new car the other day, a shiny, red sports car. As soon as I saw it in the driveway, I went over to his house because I figured he would definitely be happy today with that new sports car in his driveway. I sauntered up to his front door, rang the doorbell and waited to be greeted, for the first time ever, by the smiling face of my neighbor. He opened the door...and was frowning.

I remembered again that it's not what you do or what you have that makes you happy, it's who you are. And who you are is what you focus on. Right back to that basic universal Law of Focus: What you focus on, you find, what you focus on grows, what you focus on seems real and what you focus on, you become. Is there any "new car" in your life you are forgetting to smile about, forgetting to enjoy?

You can have any life you want. You just have to become the type of person who is supposed to have that life. That's it. The way you become that person is by focusing that way. If you want to lose weight and be healthier, focus. If you want to build your business and be a better leader, focus. If you want to build your relationship and you want it to be more passionate and sexual, focus.

Focus on the things you want in your life. You can have anything you want, if you learn to put the focus on the things you want, rather than putting your focus on the things you don't want. Then you use the unlimited power of your imagination to bring those things into your existence. That's what focus is: harnessed and disciplined imagination. So when you create that Vision and then focus on it, you'll find it.

I went into the military right after high school to learn discipline. I knew that my smarts wouldn't be enough in college without the discipline. So I knew I had to put myself in an environment that would show me how to focus. At that time, my imagination was like a big 200-pound dog that wasn't trained, and if I let it stay untrained, it would work against me.

Is your imagination untrained? Does it run wild and focus on all the wrong things? Consciously focus your imagination on what's wonderful right now and what would be wonderful. Visualize this daily, without fail, and you'll be disciplining your imagination.

Sit Without Moving, Grasshopper

"Most of the evils in life arise from man's being unable to sit still in a room."
— *Blaise Pascal*

At one point in my life, I was fortunate to work with Grand Master Jhoon Rhee. This is the man who taught Mohammed Ali how to punch and Bruce Lee how to kick. At the time, I had a hard time just sitting still. I would bounce my leg a lot. Every time I did it, Grand Master Jhoon Rhee would slap my leg. He would ask, "Do you want to shake your leg like that?" I would answer, "No." He told me to sit without moving.

He said that the ultimate fighter, the ultimate leader, the ultimate person was one who was in control of his own body. When I would shake my leg or move around, Grand Master Jhoon Rhee would reprimand me for wasting energy on useless movements instead of focusing that energy and using it to my benefit. Thanks to Grand Master Jhoon Rhee, I learned that the path to disciplining my imagination started with disciplining my physical body.

I want to share some of the exercises with you. Start by sitting down for five minutes, without moving. Don't go to sleep, don't meditate, don't watch TV, don't move. Think about whatever you want to think about, but don't move your body. Just sit down and don't move. Make the choice to sit and be still, because it's your body and your time.

If you've never done this before it's going to feel funny. You are going to itch, you're going to feel pain, but remember, it's only five minutes. Don't move your eyes, don't scratch your nose. That will be the first place the itching starts, your nose. If you scratch it, start the five minutes over. Take some deep breaths while you're sitting. The only thing you're allowed to do is breathe. Take deep breaths from your stomach, not from your chest.

Your unconscious mind will not want to sit still; it has its own agenda. Think of it as living with a big dog that has never been trained. If all of a sudden you decide that he needs to sit, stay and roll over, right now...well, that's just not going to happen without a major training effort on your part. You are in charge of your body. Train that dog.

When you can sit motionless for five minutes, the next step is to extend your control to your thoughts. Choose one thought to focus on for five minutes. If you thought controlling your body was hard, watch and see what your mind does. Out-of-the-blue thoughts are going to pop into your mind, but now, since you are able to hold your body still, you have a bit more energy to use to control your thoughts. You are sitting absolutely still, holding one thought in your mind.

It's easy to stay focused when you're in a life or death situation. What you're doing here is learning how to choose to stay focused so that you can direct your energy towards visualizing the results that you want in your life. This is not a test. There is no pass or fail.

Once you can control your thoughts for five minutes, the final exercise is to hold an image in your mind for five minutes. Sit still and hold this one image in your mind. It can be a moving image. Put yourself in this image; let it be something you are working towards. Make it bright and colorful and see it in your mind's eye as if you were looking at it physically happening right in front of you.

The most powerful manifestors in the world see their future just as you and I see through our eyes. The way they train themselves is through the process you're doing right now. Control your body, control your thoughts, and then control your imaging. Hold that image. Now that's power. That's when you are going to start seeing things happen differently. That's truly disciplining that imagination.

Your nervous system will do everything possible to produce what's on the screen in your mind: not what's on the outside, but what's on the inside. Everything on the outside is a result of what is happening with your thinking on the inside. So you must control that thinking; you must control where to focus. The only way to control your focus is to consciously direct your focus and discipline your imagination. If you leave it up to the unconscious mind, you are going to be in trouble.

You might want to challenge yourself and extend the five minute time to ten minutes, or even longer. As you continue to extend your time, you are harnessing more and more energy that you will be able to direct towards your visualizations.

Watch Your Own Cartoons

"All some students want out of school is themselves."
— poster in a classroom

Now that you know how to discipline your imagination (and you understand that it will take practice), you want to make sure that your Vision is compelling. I've mentioned before the importance of setting yourself up to win. Having a compelling Vision is setting yourself up to win as you're working on disciplining your imagination.

Once you know what you want, your imagination can help you get it because your imagination is the key that will access your entire nervous system and those hundreds of billions of brain cells in your head. But before you can get what you want, you have to have a clear and powerful Vision that you can use to keep yourself on track when your imagination wants to drift. That's why we spent so much time talking about Vision.

When my oldest son was in elementary school, his teacher called to tell me that he was having trouble staying focused. That interested me. I had often seen him sit in front of the TV and watch cartoons without moving for three hours. I wondered what the cartoons were doing that the school wasn't. I think the cartoons were using visuals and stories to engage his imagination more fully. Simply put, the cartoons were interesting. I knew that if my son was going to get more out of school, we'd have to come up with a compelling reason for him to pay attention.

Your Vision must do that for you. It must be so interesting to you that you want to put all your focus and energy towards it.

It's often hard for adults to stay focused because we don't have anything compelling enough in our lives to engage our imagination. I remember being in a movie theater watching a really intense movie. Even though the movie was good, I tore my attention away and started watching the audience. I wanted to see what this movie was doing to them. No one was moving. Everyone was focused intently on the screen.

That movie was doing a fantastic job of engaging their imagination. It was compelling enough to get them to block everything else out. That's what focus is. Focus is the ability to control your attention. That takes me back to the power of your Vision. Make sure that your Vision captures your attention and makes you want to block everything else out.

Sometimes I turn the image I'm visualizing into a story. This keeps me focused, and is one of the most powerful ways of disciplining your imagination.

Learn from a Little Dog Named Pluto

*"There are three things I always forget: names, faces, and
— I can't remember the third."*

— quote on a coffee mug

At the request of the principal, I visited a class of second grade students who had been labeled "learning disabled." I bet the teacher that I could teach the whole class to recite the planets, in order. The teacher was so certain of their learning disabled label that she took the bet right away.

I introduced myself to the students and then said, "I want you to close your eyes and see in your mind a beautiful picture." And they all closed their eyes and you could see them start to smile because they were seeing a beautiful picture. Most children are visual at that age; they're not auditory, they're visual. Their imaginations are wildly powerful, just not controlled. I was controlling their imaginations because I had them in their heads seeing pictures.

Then I said, "Now I want you to see a huge thermometer. And as this huge thermometer gets close to the Sun it explodes and Mercury comes shooting out. The first planet is Mercury." They giggled, and then I said, "Now put a beautiful woman in your picture and see her playing in the mercury. Her name is Venus. Venus is the second planet. Venus throws some of the mercury and it lands on Earth and Earth is the third planet, the one we live on." More giggling, they got that. "And now a little red faced man comes out and he's upset, he's the god of war and his name is Mars. Mars is the fourth planet.

Then the biggest planet in the universe comes out to keep order in the universe, and his name is Jupiter. Jupiter is the fifth planet. On Jupiter's shirt are the letters S-U-N, which doesn't stand for our big everyday sun, but for the next three planets. The "S" stands for Saturn, which is the sixth planet, "U" stands for Uranus, which is the seventh planet and "N" stands for Neptune, which is the eighth planet. On Jupiter's shoulder is the little dog from Disney named Pluto." I went through this whole story three times adding little details and making it bright and colorful for them. After that, every one of those kids was able to tell their teacher the names of the planets, in order.

We have to do the same things for ourselves. Many of us need a lot of visual stimulation to help us remember something. Or, maybe we need a mnemonic device — an acronym or a meaningful pattern — like I used with the students to help them recall the planets. Pictures help us see what we're saying so it's more vividly imprinted in our mind. If you experience brain mutiny, use these techniques to make your imagination work for you instead of against you.

Be Your Own Genie

"Without some goal and some effort to reach it, no man can live."
— Fyodor Dostoyevsky

Remember the TV show "I Dream of Jeannie"? Jeannie would have given Major Nelson anything he wanted, but he never asked for anything. Don't do that in your life. You are your own genie.

Don't wait for life to give you what you want. It may never happen. Ask for what you want in life. Set a goal for what you would like to achieve, establish your plan, harness the power of your imagination to create it, and then take action.

Remember, the human body contains nearly 100 million sensory receptors, allowing us to see, hear, taste, touch and smell. But the brain contains more than 10,000 billion synapses. In other words, you and I are approximately 100,000 times better equipped to experience a world that does not exist than a world that does. What this means is you can't do anything long-term that you haven't seen yourself doing in your mind's eye.

Even if you don't have the resources yet to do what you want to do, you can do it in your mind. And that's the blessing we have as human beings. We have imaginations. We have the ability to create something from nothing. We have the ability to create without any references. We have the ability to create in our mind how we want things to be.

And our unconscious mind, after it's been retrained, will do anything and everything in its power to create what we want in our lives. We'll start noticing things changing in our lives and we won't know how it happened. Phone calls will come in, people will show up, and we'll wonder, "Well, where did they come from, and why all of a sudden?" Other people will call it luck, but we'll know better.

Try This at Home —
Questions, Suggestions, and Action Plans

To Explore

- Why is it important that you discipline your thoughts and your imagination?

- What will you gain by getting your mind under control?

- What will you lose if you don't do this?

To Act

- Daydream about what you want instead of letting bad dreams ruin your day.

- Make your daydreams exciting! See yourself in bright, bold colors with full sound and movement.

- Do the sit still exercise!

To Remember

- To strengthen your mind you must train it, just as you would do for your body.

- Your power of focus has to be developed by consistently and consciously disciplining your imagination.

- Your past does not equal your future.

NOTES

I don't think of all the misery but of the beauty that still remains.

— Anne Frank

NOTES

A man cannot be comfortable without his own approval.

— Mark Twain

Select Role Models

My grandfather was a giant of a man.

When he walked, the earth shook.

When he laughed, the birds fell out of the trees.

His hair caught fire from the sun.

His eyes were patches of sky.

— Eth Clifford

CHAPTER 5

Why Not Write Your Own Starring Role?

"Few is the number who think with their own minds and feel with their own hearts."

— Albert Einstein

Remember earlier in the book when I jokingly suggested to someone who was grousing about everything that was wrong with his life that he sell his life story to Hollywood?

Well, there's power in seeing your life as a movie. It's a rich metaphor for examining who's directing, who's writing the script...and are we a main character or an extra in our own lives?

Picture your life as a motion picture. Who wrote the script you're following? Until now, there have been many people writing your script for you: your parents, your teachers, other relatives, authority figures, friends, acquaintances, the media, significant emotional events of your life...everyone and everything except you. It's time to take the motion picture of your life and turn it into a box office sensation. It's time for you to use your head and your heart to diagram the movie of your life.

You may be wondering, "Where and how am I going to get started?" Well, I'm going to show you.

Be the Cheetah

"Children have never been good at listening to their parents, but they have never failed to imitate them."

— James Baldwin

I remember being fascinated by a TV special on cheetahs. In one segment they showed how the baby cheetahs learned to hunt for food. The mother was out stalking her prey, and the baby cheetahs were close enough to watch her, but far enough away to be out of danger. After the excitement was over and the family was feasting on the dinner mom brought home, the kids began to play. And guess what they were playing? That's right, they were playing "let's go hunting." They were acting out exactly what they saw their mother doing when she was stalking and bringing down her prey. They were imitating her behavior, and that is how they learn to hunt and survive.

As humans, we do the same thing. As babies we learn how to walk, how to talk, and how to behave by watching the people around us and then modeling our behavior after that of others. I know for a fact that my children model more of what I do than what I say. My kids watch me. They watch me when I don't think they're watching, that's when they're learning the most. Our kids learn by watching and evaluating what we do, whether we want them to or not. Even as we get older, we continue to emulate what we see around us in life and in leisure. And often we don't recognize what is happening, sometimes with unfortunate results.

Whom Are You Modeling Yourself After?

"We are all looking for someone who will make us do what we can."
— Ralph Waldo Emerson

Here's an example of a person getting himself into a situation where he didn't even realize he was influenced by a role model he himself was providing. There was a fantasy game that was really popular a number of years ago called *Dungeons and Dragons*. It's a game for which you really need your imagination. The players in the game each take on the persona of a different character, and there's always a dungeon master. Each character has his own powers and strengths, and the characters need to work together to complete a mission. The game can last for weeks, as long as there are enough characters left alive in the game to continue the journey.

One of my friends was in a group of gamers who were playing *Dungeons and Dragons*. This guy was quite shy, even a little bit cowardly...OK, he was actually a big coward. People would push him around and he'd just laugh it off and say it didn't bother him. I don't know what happened to him to make him so passive, but he was a real introvert. He was also really smart, so I enjoyed hanging out with him, even though he was quiet.

One day, someone brought this game into our barracks and a few people started to play. When "shy guy" got in the game, he picked a character who had a personality that was opposite his own. In the game he was a warrior with a double-edged ax who would be the first one to attack the monsters. I never knew exactly what "reckless abandon" meant until I saw how he played this game.

My friend's group would stay up all night playing the game. He loved it. He talked about it all the time and really "came alive" when he'd discuss strategy and what had happened the night before.

After about two weeks of playing this game, an interesting thing happened. "Shy guy" began to act like his character in his real life. If someone pushed him, he'd push back. He started getting more vocal and more aggressive. He gained confidence and even asked a girl out and started dating.

Everything was going great until "shy guy's" character in the game was killed. As soon as that happened, "shy guy" lost all his confidence and got really depressed. He regressed back into being his "old self," and his grades started falling.

Back then, I didn't understand why he fell apart like that and I didn't know what to do about it. I wish I knew then what I know now because I think I might have been able to help him.

Now I understand that game gave him "permission" to act tough. When he was playing his *Dungeons and Dragons* character, he didn't have to be himself (shy and weak), he could be more assertive and forceful. He actually took on the persona of his character in both the game and in life.

When his character died, he no longer had permission to act the way his character did. He had to go back to being himself — and that old submissive self was a bummer after having been a confident guy who went after what he wanted and who was comfortable in his own skin.

What's the moral of this story? "Shy guy" needed that game to shed his old self and become more of the person he wanted to be. But you don't need a game to make yourself over. You have this program. In 45 days, you can shed your old habits that are keeping you locked in a persona that no longer suits you. By taking this challenge, you too can be stronger, more assertive, and more confident by the end of next month. You can be the person you want to be, and you don't have to play Dungeons and Dragons to make it happen.

No More Excuses

"One of the toughest things to learn is the ability to make yourself do the thing you have to do, when it ought to be done, whether you like it or not."
— *Thomas Henry Huxley*

I hear a lot of excuses for why people can't change. The one I hear the most is, "That's just who I am." Now what the heck does that mean? I always want to ask those people if they thoughtfully and deliberately decided who they were going to be. Of course, I don't ask this, because I don't want to get into any fist fights, but if you have the courage, ask yourself that question.

So many people are walking around living out scripts that other people wrote for them and claiming that it's just who they are. Nonsense. It's not you. If it's hurting you, or if it's keeping you from your desires, then it's not you. If it's getting in the way of you living a healthy, fulfilled, happy life, then it's not you.

If I bought you a lifetime pass to a really bad movie, a movie that made you feel bad every time you watched it, would you keep going to see that movie just because I gave you a lifetime pass for it? It's true that you don't know if you'll like the movie playing in the next theater, but there's only one way to find out, right? Even if you feel uncomfortable trying something new, it is worth your while to try it.

We all have certain habits or traits that are keeping us from getting what we really want in life. The difference between the happy people and the people who are not getting what they want out of life is that the happy people are willing to change and the other people refuse to get rid of those parts that are holding them back. They think that the world is supposed to bend to fit them; after all this is how God made them, right?

Don't allow yourself to agree with that thinking. God gives you desires: desires to be more, to have closer relationships, to do more, and to have more. I don't think God gives you a desire and then creates you so that there is no way you can reach that desire.

Often when people disagree with me on this point, they claim, "I believe people are born with their own unique characteristics and their own unique gifts and talents." I agree. We all are unique and we are born with incredible gifts and talents that are unique to us. The thing is that we seldom use them; we seldom get around to noticing what they are.

I'm reminded of certain areas of cities where, statistically speaking, very few people make it out of those neighborhoods, which often plagued with high crime rates, poor educational systems, and little opportunity. What's happening there? It's not that the people who live in such places aren't unique; it's that they pick up their destructive habits and attitudes through imitation. We all grow up emulating the people around us and then defining ourselves by those exact habits and attitudes that we adopted.

Most of us did not choose the habits and attitudes we took on as children. Hopefully, as we mature, we start to drop the habits and attitudes that we don't like and then create ones we do like. But no one tells us to do that. We each have to find our own path. So give yourself permission to change now. And then start changing by noticing leaders whom you can model your new habits after in constructive, empowering ways.

Don't Re-Invent the Wheel

"Teachers affect eternity. Who knows where their influence will end?"

— *Henry Brooks Adams*

We all know what it looks like when someone is trying to be something he isn't, right?

That is not what following a role model is about; it is not about pretending to be something you're not. Nor is it about reinventing the wheel. Whatever your dreams or goals, chances are there is already someone who is good at what you need to learn.

Who is someone you respect? Is it a business owner who started her own company and is now a successful entrepreneur? Is it a friend who is always kind and compassionate? Is it a parent who models integrity? Is it a teacher who encouraged you and believed in your potential?

Figure out what you want to do and who you want to be, and then identify someone who is a walking-talking role model of that. Find people who have already succeeded in the areas you want to work on. Take the best of what they've learned and adapt their actions and beliefs to your own life. Apply their approach and principles and integrate them into your life. Why start from scratch when other people have already paved the way and you can fast-forward your success by learning from their examples?

We all have role models, whether they are people we're consciously imitating or people we're unconsciously imitating because we spend so much of our time with them. That's why we need to be careful about who we hang out with. Are the people in your crowd modeling helpful behaviors or hurtful behaviors? Great people have learned how to deliberately model their behavior after individuals who will accelerate their best self. The most talented singers in the world have role models they look up to and admire. The greatest athletes in the world follow the example of champions in their sport so they can fast-forward their performances. The best business leaders and the greatest political leaders all have respected role models whom they turn to for advice in how to handle challenging situations.

Who are your role models? Name a role model at work, at home, and in the community who is a walking-talking example of the qualities you want for yourself. How can you increase the amount of time you spend with this person so her excellent influence "rubs off" on you?

Combine Your Mother and Evil Kneivel

"I pretended to be somebody I wanted to be until finally I became that person. Or he became me."

— *Cary Grant*

There's one final, important step you need to take before you get into deliberately modeling your behavior and patterns on those of positive role models: you have to identify all the roles you play in your own life. When anyone asks me, "Who are you?" I tell the person that I'm a lot of things; I'm a lot of people. Which "me" are you talking about? This is why my life will never be boring. I can never be bored because there are so many "me's" in here. People worry about me and all my personalities. I just say, "Yep, that's me. I've got a bunch of them." You can have fun that way.

In your own life, you play many roles. Look at yourself as being a one-person play. Have you ever seen a one-woman or one-man show? That one person has to go into character for each different persona that she's playing in the show. I've seen some magnificent one-person shows.

Your life is that same way: you are a one-person show. You play many roles: you're a parent, you're a spouse, you're a daughter, you're a son; you're a brother, you're a sister, you're a friend, you're a cousin; you're a nutritionist, you're a lawyer, you're a wealth weaver. You are so many things, and you're playing many of these roles at the same time. When you are consciously aware of the many roles that you play in your life, you can easily see what specifically you want to model. Each role that you play may need a different role model. Having a clearly defined role for each one that you are modeling yourself after will also help you form the questions that you'll need to ask in order to emulate these roles effectively.

If there's one mistake that people most often make in this stage, it's that they think should model themselves after all aspects of a person. Instead they need to decipher just what will help and what may hurt, and take to themselves only the elements that will help. Selecting parts of role models carefully helps assure that you don't get the prizes you were looking for, while hurting yourself in other areas of your life. If you see someone behaving in destructive ways, then consciously choose not to be around that person and be clear that you do NOT want to copy that aspect of his behavior.

My mother is a wonderful role model for being a parent, but modeling my behavior after hers won't help me be a business president. She's the best mother I've ever seen, and a great friend, but if I'm looking for resources to help me excel at running my business, she's not the one I'd want to emulate. So, just because she's a great person doesn't mean that I can model myself after all parts of her and expect to excel in every area of my life.

Most people think of Evil Kneivel as a daredevil stunt driver who took incredible risks as he jumped across canyons or rode a motorcycle over a long row of trucks in Las Vegas. Looking more closely, I noticed how very safety conscious he was. Using him as a role model, I can embrace his showmanship and his calculated caution without having to adopt his choice in profession.

We all have a different cast of roles for our own life, so we need to emulate different people. Choose people role models based on your own roles. Figure out everything in your life that you want and the roles you have to play in order to bring those elements into your life.

Also, think about the roles you are already playing in life and find people you admire in those areas who are getting what you want. If what you see seems wholesome and is helping other people, and not hurting them, mimic it. As Cary Grant pointed out, if you pretend to be the person you want to be, you can become that person.

Get Help from Alexander the Great — or Your Dad

"I give my dad credit for single-handedly keeping my math grades high enough so I wouldn't be held back in school."

— *Steven Spielberg*

That's enough explanation about modeling yourself after others. Here's how you do it. You have already consciously determined what roles you play in your life and where you can get specific help from role models. Now you need to know exactly what result you're looking for within each role. After you've chosen which characteristics you want to emulate, the next step is to find a person to model yourself after for each of your main roles in life.

I'm going to say something that may surprise you. The role model you choose can be either real or imaginary. By imaginary, I mean a character from a book, movie or TV show, or it could be an ideal that you create in your mind. That's the power of a good book, movie, or TV show. You can read about Harry Potter, and say, "I want to be resourceful like that." You can watch a movie such as Braveheart and say, "I want to have courage like that." You may not ever meet Harry or Mel Gibson, but just watching them gives you an image of how you want to be.

After you've chosen your role model, there are three specific aspects of that person that you want to emulate: beliefs, physiology and strategy. The place you want to start is with your beliefs, because beliefs go a long way in controlling your focus, and you know that what you focus on, you find, what you focus on grows, what you focus on seems real and what you focus on, you become. So, controlling your focus is extremely important.

A second reason that it's important to understand beliefs first is that every strategy is born from a belief. I'll understand and therefore be able to use a strategy much more effectively when I know the "why's" that went into formulating the strategy. I will also be able to make the strategy fit my specific situation because I understand how it works; I'm not just relying on following a step-by-step plan that falls apart when something unexpected comes up.

So you always want to start with the beliefs. You can find out someone's beliefs by simply asking him: "What do you believe about religion, about health, about leadership, about service, or about (fill in the blank)?" Then ask: "How did you come to think that? Are there exceptions to that? What would you do if you were in my shoes? What motivates you to feel that way?" Your mindset at this point should be one of curiosity; questions will just come to you in that state.

If I had a problem with anger and I wanted to stay calm, I would find my role model and ask him, "When people are yelling at you, what do you say to yourself that allows you to respond calmly? What do you focus on? What is it that specifically allows you to keep your cool under fire?"

There is no formula for asking questions; just develop a curious mindset and keep your outcome in mind. If you're modeling yourself after characters or ideals, you can probably pick up on some of their beliefs from their dialogue, but mostly you'll have to use your imagination to predict what they believe, what they focus on, and their other secrets to success.

I have certain role models, such as Alexander the Great, whom I've never met. But by reading their stories and using my imagination, I can get to know the way they think. I even have a ring with Alexander the Great on it because I love the resolve, faith, and drive he brought to his leadership. He also has certain traits I wouldn't want to adopt, which is one of the great things about modeling ourselves after someone. We can choose only those traits we want to emulate and overlook the rest.

The next thing you want to emulate is physiology. Energy comes from presence, from how you carry and use your body, so focus on your role models' physiology. How do they carry themselves? What are they doing with their shoulders, their expressions, their gestures? How do they walk? How do they sit? Do they lean in when they're listening to someone? Do they hold eye contact? Get curious.

The final thing you want to do is emulate your role models' success strategies. What are the specific steps they take to get the outcome? What resources do they have in place? How do they go about scheduling the events? Get the step-by-step process, but remember to always understand the organizing principles, or beliefs, that go with the strategy. If you come across a strategy or a step that you don't fully understand, start back with eliciting the specific beliefs around that strategy or step.

Invite Yourself to the Round Table

"The wisdom of the wise and the experience of the ages are perpetuated by quotations."
— *Benjamin Disraeli*

Here's something else you can do to help yourself: Read biographies and study great philosophers such as Albert Einstein, Martin Luther King and Henry David Thoreau. That's one of the reasons I've used so many quotes from great thinkers in this book: to prompt you to look more deeply into their thoughts and words. By reading their pearls of wisdom, we have access to people we've never met and to profound thoughts that might otherwise never have occurred to us.

I love to read biographies because I feel like I get to know these people from the inside out. I discover what they believed, how they thought, and why they acted the way they did.

I access their wisdom to accelerate my own. When I need to figure something out in my own life, I use my imagination to create a panel of these experts. I'll sit in front of this panel of great thinkers and ask them, "What would you guys do in this situation?" Imagining their answers produces some amazing insights that I'd never be able to come up with on my own.

Your brain is so magnificent. If you fill it with enough good information, and then ask it a question, it will process all that good information and come up with a great answer. Of course, if you put in bad information, that will also shape the quality of your answer.

Are you going through a tough time right now? Are you facing a challenging decision and you're not sure what to do? Create your own panel of experts. Ask them for help. Imagine how they would solve your situation. The more time you spend studying the lives of great thinkers, the more you will be able to learn from their positive example. That's one of the many wonderful benefits of reading, whether it's an "old-fashioned book" from the library or an entry on the web. You can access this valuable wisdom for free. And remember, while you're modeling yourself after these experts and learning how they got to where they are, they in turn got to where they were by modeling themselves after other leaders.

You Are the Company You Keep

"We should learn from the mistakes of others. We don't have time to make them all ourselves."
— *Groucho Marx*

I'm teaching you here how to consciously model yourself after the people who are already where you want to be in life, but the truth is that you already know how to do this, and you're doing it all the time. A word of caution — there are three main ways to change your identity: by experiencing momentous emotional events (both good and traumatic), through conditioning and repetition (which we've talked about in breaking and building habits), and by embracing your environment and peer group (because you will model yourself after the people you choose to be around). On an unconscious level, if you are not deliberately choosing your actions and attitudes, you will model yourself after the people you spend the most time with.

Have you ever heard the saying, "Only hang around people you'd like to be like."? Well, that's what I'm saying here. Make sure your peer group consists of people who think and act the way you want to think and act. If they don't, change your peer group. I know that sounds harsh. It's just that you will acquire the characteristics of the people you spend time with. If you want to be wealthy, hang out with wealthy people. When you hang out with rich people you begin to unconsciously emulate their attitudes and actions which helps you reap "rich" results.

Beware. The same thing happens if you hang out with trouble-makers. The same thing happens if you hang out with complainers who are always griping about what's wrong with their life. Either you are unconsciously choosing to emulate people you decide to be around, or they are emulating you. Either way, make sure your friends are positive rather than negative influences.

Turn Your Life into an Unsinkable Submarine

"I'm tough. I'm indestructible. I'm like the coyote in "Road Runner" who was always getting flattened and dynamited and crushed and in the next scene is strolling along, completely normal again."

— *Betsy Byars*

Have you ever been so upset about something that you couldn't function in any area of your life? Did it help to be totally inca-pacitated? What most people don't know because they've never been able to experience it, is that if you can keep the problems in one area of your life from affecting all other areas of your life, then you will heal faster. What I'm going to give you here is a gift that will affect your life forever.

Look at your life as if it were a submarine. A submarine has many different compartments that are connected, just as your life has many different roles that are connected. What happens, though, if the submarine is hit by a missile that cuts a hole in the side of the sub? Does the submarine immediately fill with water and sink? No, because a submarine has a built in failsafe that allows each compartment to be closed off from the rest of the sub if anything happens. It has water-tight integrity; if any compartment is compromised, it is locked away. It has to be locked away so that the rest of the boat can thrive and accomplish its mission.

You want to do the same thing with your life. You never want to allow a challenge in one role to become pervasive and sink your entire life. If you let a problem in one area of your life become pervasive, it can do permanent damage. You never want to get into such a situation.

That's why understanding that you play different roles in life, and knowing what those roles are, is so important. I have to know how to switch roles so that no matter what happens at my job, when I get home, I can still be a fully present, loving husband and father. No matter what kind of negative thing happens in one area of my life, I keep it confined to that role. That's giving integrity to my life. That's saying that I care about each area of my life enough to not let problems in one area sink my whole life.

If I don't figure out how to do that, then when I have trouble at work, it will impact my kids, my wife, my eating habits, my workout schedule, my hobbies...my whole life. I've seen so many people with work problems or relationship problems who can't get themselves to eat right, or work out, or socialize. When you define your roles and what you want in your life for each of those roles, you can keep trouble from being pervasive.

I have clients who call me and say, "I'm so messed up," or "I'm so depressed," or "I'm so down." And I always ask them, "Which you?" And they shout back, "What do you mean 'which me,'? Just me." What I'm getting at is that we all play so many roles; in the area of relationships, for example, I'm a father, I'm a husband, I'm a friend, I'm a son, I'm a lover, I'm a nephew, and I'm an uncle. Which "me" is feeling screwed up or depressed or down?

You see, even though we may feel bad about one role in our life, we have so many other roles that we can feel great about, but we don't think about all our roles, we only think about the squeaky one that we're feeling bad about at the moment. I want my clients to see that there is so much more than one role in their life. That's how you keep challenges and problems in perspective: you see that your life is so much bigger than this one role, and with all the resources of this unlimited you at your disposal, surely you are going to figure out a solution to your problem.

You also know that you are better at playing some roles in your life than you are at playing others. When challenges come up in life, you need to go into the role where you are strong and have momentum instead of allowing that one challenge to be pervasive and sink your whole life. Use the strength and resources that you have in that role to help you heal the problem you are experiencing in another role. Letting problems control your life is like giving attention to the bad kids and ignoring the good kids. The good kids will become bad to get attention. Remember that.

A 24-Hour-a-Day Job

"There is only one thing that remains to us, that cannot be taken away: to act with courage and dignity and to stick to the ideals that give meaning to your life."
— *Jawaharlal Nehru*

Let's review. First of all, you have to understand that the role modeling mechanism is working 24 hours a day; you're always modeling yourself after someone or some idea. In any type of situation, you are either unconsciously modeling yourself after some other person or he is unconsciously modeling himself after you. Whoever has the most certainty will be the person being emulated. Second, you have to give yourself permission to consciously build or improve the model you select. You have to give yourself permission to change. When you give yourself that permission to change and start to consciously use the modeling mechanism, you will start to see changes in your life.

We talked about how you have to know the roles that you live in your life so that you can give life and integrity to each role that you play, and so that you can start pinpointing what you need to focus on in your life to get the results that you're looking for. There will be some results that you want to see in your life that you don't have a role for yet.

For example, if you're living hand-to-mouth and you want to be wealthy, you will need to create some roles for yourself, such as the role of the investor, the role of the budgeter, and the role of the estate planner. You have to create those roles. You have to start developing new roles in your life if you want to go to a higher level. It works well to give your roles names that are exciting to you. So, instead of being an "investor" you might be a "wealth weaver." Call it anything that makes you want to live that role and live it well.

Once you've defined your roles and what you want most for yourself in each of those roles, start modeling yourself after the roles' positive aspects. Why make the mistakes all on your own when you can save yourself years of effort by learning from the mistakes and wise choices already made by other people? Keep in mind that it is your responsibility and your obligation to find the people who are getting the things in life that you want, and to learn how to model yourself after those particular people. It's your responsibility and no one else's.

I'm very excited about the distinctions you can get from this information, and I want you to go back and think about the things we're talking about here. Whatever you do doesn't have to be perfect. Remember that this program is a beginning. These are things you can work on for the rest of your life to continue growing, and as you grow you'll need to play even bigger and more powerful roles to get to that next level. So, please look at the different roles you can play, look at where you allow situations to sink the whole ship when only one role is submerged.

One final question about role models and your life: are you being the best role model you can be? Are you acting with courage? Are you sticking to the ideals that give meaning to your life and to the lives of the people who are around you? We never know how the little things we do impact other people. Let's make sure even those little things count.

Try This at Home —
Questions, Suggestions, and Action Plans

To Explore

- Why is it important that you learn to effectively model yourself after others?

- What will you gain by doing this?

- What will you lose if you don't do this?

To Act

- For any goal you want to achieve or any attitude that you want to develop, ask yourself whom you can model yourself after. Think about that person's beliefs, language and physical expression.

- Create your own round table. What characteristics and qualities would most support you in getting to your Vision? Who already owns these traits? Add those people to your round table.

- Define the roles that you need to adopt to get the results you want in every area of your life.

- Exercise your curiosity about the people around you that you do and don't already know.

- Ask great questions of the people you're already in a relationship with, get to know them even better.

To Remember

- You are already modeling yourself after others all the time. Consciously choose what specific qualities you are going to emulate from different people.

- Who you spend consistent time with is who you become. Choose to spend time with people you'd like to be like. When you find yourself spending time with people who are not the best role models, choose to consciously be a role model for them.

- Don't allow challenges to be pervasive when only one role is impacted. Practice switching roles and focusing only on what you'd like to have happen in that role in that moment.

NOTES

The family fireside is the best of schools.

— Arnold H. Glasow

NOTES

What would life be if we had no courage to attempt anything?
— Vincent van Gogh

Take Intelligent Risks

An individual dies when instead of taking risks

and hurling himself toward being,

he cowers within, and takes refuge there.

— E. M. Cioran

CHAPTER 6

It's Time to Walk the Talk

"To be courageous...requires no exceptional qualifications, no magic formula, no special combination of time, place, and circumstance. It is an opportunity that sooner or later is presented to us all."
— *John F. Kennedy*

I know you've been working hard to make changes and really grow in your life. You've created a Vision, you've broken old habits, and you've conditioned new ones. You've learned how to focus your imagination, and you've cut years off your learning curve by selecting role models. You've also learned a lot about how the unconscious mind works and about the universal laws that run the world.

The next step is to trust your growth and all that you've learned. It's time to step outside your comfort zone and start taking intelligent risks. Life is going to bring change; I'm sure you've already noticed that. The only way to position yourself to appreciate that change and benefit from it is to learn how to step outside of your comfort zone intelligently. If you don't take the first step, you'll end up waiting to see what happens in your life and then going into reaction mode. If you don't take that first step, you may spend your whole life pretending you feel safe and secure forever and have an OK life.

But I don't think that's good enough for you. I know that an "OK" life is not OK with you. I know you're ready to take some risks.

Survive a Hurricane

"If you want to conquer fear, don't sit at home and think about it. Get out and get busy."
— *Dale Carnegie*

I'm not talking about going bungee-jumping without a bungee. Or skydiving without a parachute. Or going to Vegas and putting all your money on Red-12. No, I'm not talking about that. I'm talking about gathering the courage to do the things that you really want to do with your life. Things you know you can do.

What would you do if you knew that a killer hurricane was on its way? You know you should be proactive and leave when you get the warning that the hurricane is coming.

But there will always be people who don't want to leave because they're too afraid. They don't want to pack up and go somewhere new. They're comfortable in their home and maybe, just maybe, their house will be fine. It's the same way in life. Change will come at you with hurricane force. And let's be honest with ourselves, if we would choose to look at our lives objectively, with awareness, we'd see the change on the horizon most of the time.

That's when you need to take action: when the change is out there on the horizon, when it's still small. That's called being proactive.

When you choose to be proactive, you'll be able to benefit from the change when it happens. If you choose to keep your eyes off the horizon so you can pretend that you don't know change is coming, then when it comes, and it will, you'll be forced to deal with it reactively, in crisis mode.

There are three types of people. The first type of person, I call the Proactors; they decide to change before they are forced to. The second type of person are the Reactors; they wait until life is about to flatten them, and then they change. And the third type of person are the Stagnators; they refuse to change and end up getting buried by the changes that happen in their lives.

Proactors are wacky. I've been called wacky all my life, and I love it. I've always done things before I had to do them (except maybe my college term papers, but that doesn't count). If you could persuade me that something would help me later, help me have a great life, help me have more of something, I did it. Even when things were already great in my life. If my relationship was great, I'd look at making it even better. If I had enough money, I'd ask myself how I could make more, how could I invest more? I'm always looking to take every part of my life to the next level.

See, we're put here on earth to create. That simply means that we're always looking to grow and expand, even if it's only on an unconscious level. If we're not growing and expanding, we won't feel fulfilled. But there are two ways to grow, right? You can grow by struggling your way through whatever life throws at you, or you can grow by leaving your comfort zone before life circumstances force you to leave it. If you choose not to be proactive, life will provide you with certain lessons to help you along, and those lessons aren't always pleasant. Either way, you're going to grow, so why not have fun doing it by being the Proactor?

Remember when you were a kid and you just couldn't wait to grow up and get bigger and stronger? It was so exciting, you not only looked forward to it, but you did everything you could to hurry the process along. Remember?

Somewhere along the way, you lost that excitement. You were disappointed, or hurt, one too many times and you began to stay where you were comfortable to protect yourself. Well, your feet can't grow if you keep forcing them into the shoe size that you've been wearing since you were six years old. You've got to get bigger shoes if you want your feet to keep growing. You need to do that with your life also. You need to get bigger dreams and then give yourself the tools and the permission to go after those dreams.

Check in with your thinking. Look at your habits, examine your goals. Ask yourself, "How can I improve, and what's the next level for me?" Become aware of what's happening in your life, and look at that in relation to where you want to be in your life. Now be proactive and make your Vision happen. And people will look at you as if you're wacky or just lucky, but that's no big deal.

If you're not proactive, then chances are that you're in the habit of being the Reactor (I'd place a strong bet that you're not in the Stagnator category of refusing to change). And that's all right, because now that you know this is a habit, you can change it. You already know how to do that.

Here's how the Reactors handle life. Their wives are about to leave them, so they change. They're on drugs, they're about to die, so they change. They go broke, so they change. Their husbands walk out, so they change. They lose their jobs, so they change. And life does reward those people: they can get on Oprah, and they can turn their story into the ABC movie of the week. The magic of changing from Saul to Paul, right? Take the story of Ebenezer Scrooge. We love that. And that's why we unconsciously train ourselves to do that. We want the significance of being noticed for making such a dramatic change just when everything seemed so hopeless. So we wait until everything is about to fall apart. We wait until our health is gone, or we've declared bankruptcy, or our spouse and children have left. We do it unconsciously so that we can be called a hero when we turn everything around.

Sounds good...so why would you want to become the Proactor when you have all those rewards waiting for you as the Reactor? By comparison, the life of the Proactor seems boring; no drama. The truth is that the proactive people run the world. The proactive people are the happiest, the most fulfilled, and have the most joy. There's plenty of room for all that happiness, fulfillment, and joy when you get rid of the drama.

For the sake of completeness, I'll tell you a little bit about that third group, the Stagnators, the ones who aren't going to change no matter what happens. These are the people who won't leave their house even when the hurricane is right over them. They're unwilling to change. They're unwilling to adjust. They're unwilling to open their mind to new beliefs, new actions and new results.

These people can look at their lives and see that they're not where they want to be, but instead of changing, they'd rather fall back on "Well, that's how I was raised." Well, maybe how you were raised doesn't serve you anymore; maybe it was just a tradition being passed from generation to generation. If it's not getting the result you need, then you need to look at new options. That's all I'm going to say about that.

Get Ready for Success

*"What God has intended for you goes far beyond
anything you can imagine."*

— Oprah Winfrey

You now have the opportunity to step out and be the new you,
the real you. The first thing you want to do is to be intelligent
about the risks that you're going to take. I don't want you to do
anything out of pure excitement alone. I want you to think about
what you're choosing to do.

Ask yourself, "What would I have to do to reach my Vision?" If
you're thinking about a specific action, ask yourself, "Does this
action fit with my Vision and my goals?" If it will harm you or
kill you, don't do it. I don't want people calling me from the
hospital. I'm not talking about that kind of risk.

Put yourself into that uncertain place where you know there is a
risk associated with your Vision. Everything you want and attain
is driven by your Vision. If you don't have the competence to do
something that you need to do to reach your Vision, then ask
yourself, "Where can I learn that skill? Who can I emulate?"

After you've decided upon the actions that you need to take, the
next step is to develop a plan. Develop a plan to the best of your
ability. No one can ask for anything more than that: the best of
your ability.

When you've developed a plan to the best of your ability, then go
for it. The resources that you need (and the ones that you don't
even know you need) will be provided, courtesy of your unconscious mind. Do your part, to the best of your ability, and the rest
will come your way. The people you need to help you will be
attracted into your life. Why? Because that's just the way life
works.

Next ask yourself, "Am I ready to deal with the consequences,
either way?" Are you ready to deal with getting what you want in
your life and are you prepared to deal with not getting it just yet?

The bottom line is that if you are looking to happily achieve, instead of achieving to be happy, then you're probably ready. If you're looking at stepping outside of your comfort zone as an opportunity to grow and to learn and to see what you're capable of becoming, then you're probably ready. If you're holding your breath or waiting to see what happens before you decide if you're happy or if you're worthy, then you need to stop and re-examine your beliefs. Know that your Creator will never put you in a situation that you can't handle.

As funny as it sounds, one of your challenges may be dealing with success. I know in my life I was ready to deal with the failures, but when the successes started happening, I had to hold on to keep myself from freaking out.

You have to be able to deal with the success, just as well as you deal with the failure. When you attract that pretty girl, don't freak out. Don't freak out when you attract the guy who has every quality on your list. Don't freak out when you land your dream job. Realize that you're worthy of it. Are you willing to deal with the consequences either way?

Take the Next Step

"To play it safe is not to play."

— *Robert Altman*

How do you step out of your comfort zone? How do you expand who you are? How do you tap into the courage you have inside of you? It's all about attitude. You control your attitude by controlling what you focus on. Focus on what you're going to gain by stepping out of your comfort zone. Focus on who you're going to become, what you're going to do, and how you're going to grow. Focus on those you're going to be able to help.

Use your imagination. See yourself boldly doing the things you want to do. See yourself taking different actions. See yourself doing things differently. See yourself having fun with your life and being playful, instead of playing it safe.

Next, you have to manage your self-talk. What are you saying to yourself, out loud and in your head? You have to encourage yourself, reminding yourself why you're committed to growing and what your life is going to be like on the other side of all the hard work.

When you feel down, remind yourself that it's just a feeling and that you can change the feeling by shifting your focus, your self-talk, and your physiology. Ask yourself great questions. Repeat empowering incantations: "I've trained it, now I'll trust it. All the faith I need is within me now." Design your own incantations that you can repeat to yourself throughout the day: when you're walking from the parking lot, while you're shaving or putting on makeup, or while you're waiting in line or in the elevator.

Let Them Call You a Gambler

"It gets late early out there."

— *Yogi Berra*

I left the Navy after serving for 11 years. I still remember how I felt before and after I made the decision to leave. The Navy was all I knew at that point. Everything I had learned about being a man, I had learned in the Navy. When I told people I was getting out, they looked at me as if I was crazy. In their eyes, I had everything going for me, and my future in the Navy looked great.

But I had to listen to my Vision. I realize that, as John Wayne used to say, I was burning daylight. Time was passing and I knew in my heart that I wasn't doing what I wanted to do.

I had to listen to my calling and take that first step. And I'll tell you, taking that first step is scarier than actually being outside the comfort zone. Because once you get out, you see how refreshing it is. It's so amazing. You get a chance to see who you really are. If you want a chance to see your gifts, step outside your comfort zone.

Everyone around me thought I was a crazy risk taker, gambling with my future. But I was just being proactive, and proactive people are actually the most security-minded people on earth. We know that the world is changing. We know that we have to adapt and adjust both our actions and our ways of thinking. We know that we have to anticipate change. So we're really very security-minded.

The truly secure path is growth. If you want certainty in your life, you attain it by selectively initiating change in your life. You get it by stepping out into uncertainty before you have to. It's called "taking risks" only because the immediate result is uncertain, and by stepping out before you absolutely have to, you allow yourself the luxury of time. If the result is not exactly what you had planned, you still have time to change your approach and try something different. You don't want to be pushed out into uncertainty; you want to step out on your own. That's what growth is.

What allowed me to step into a world of uncertainty and leave the Navy was internal certainty. This program is helping you to develop your own internal certainty. The reason you have to work to develop internal certainty is that we're taught to look outside ourselves to get certainty. We're conditioned to find certainty in our careers, our relationships, our money and our possessions.

Once something is conditioned, our unconscious minds take over to keep things the same. Remember your unconscious mind works subjectively. It's not interested in growing; it's interested in certainty and sameness. That's how it helps you survive. So our unconscious mind says, "Great. Stay here. Yes, it's abusive, but stay anyway. You're not getting what you want out of life, but at least you feel certain."

But that type of certainty is an illusion. The only true certainty is internal certainty. You grow your internal certainty by trusting your ability to grow and to expand and to be flexible, and by trusting in the way that the universe works: according to principle. You know the main principles: the Law of Control, the Law of Attraction, the Four-Part Law of Focus, and the Law of Belief. Trust in what you know to be true in your heart. That is not gambling.

Set Your Own Thermostat

"Even if you're on the right track, you'll still get run over if you just sit there."

— *Mark Twain*

We all have a thermostat set for each area of our lives: our health, our relationships, our career...every area. If the thermostat is set for 75, but you've been slacking off and the indicator drops to 65, you'll kick yourself into action so you can get back to that 75 mark. If you've really been working hard and the indicator rises to 85, you'll start to sabotage your success because your identity says you belong at 75, not 85. The bottom line is that you're going to do what you have to do to keep yourself at 75. You're not living the life you want, but you're comfortable.

I remember learning to play golf. I already saw myself as an athlete so I thought I could just teach myself. I developed my own swing and everything, and I could really hit the ball far even if I couldn't always control the direction. When I finally took lessons, the pro told me that my grip was messed up. He showed me how to grip the club, but when I tried to hit the ball using the grip he showed me, the ball didn't go anywhere. Besides that, the new grip was really uncomfortable. I just wanted to go back to my old grip.

The pro asked me how good a golfer I wanted to be. Well, of course I wanted to be great. He told me not to worry about the results I was getting right now, and to just practice swinging with my new grip. So I practiced and I practiced, and soon I started to hit the ball a long way, but it was still uncomfortable. So I kept practicing.

Finally, the pro took me off the driving range and onto the golf · course. I had on my new golf shoes and my new outfit, and I was ready to play. I walked onto the golf course and everyone was watching me. I started to feel really uncomfortable, and then I started wondering what all these people were thinking about me. So I was feeling uncomfortable as I was about to take my first swing with this uncomfortable grip.

What do you think I did? Did I stick with the new grip, or did I go back to my old grip? Yep, I went back to my old grip, because that felt more comfortable in the moment. It felt certain in the moment. What result do you think I got? Did I get the result I wanted: to feel comfortable and accepted? No, I almost hit someone in the head with my wild shot.

It doesn't pay to always be comfortable. You may think you're on the right track, but if you've been on the same track for a l-o-n-g time, chances are you're just sitting there, and you're not making progress. After I had worked with the new uncomfortable golf grip long enough, it became comfortable. You have to be willing to set your thermostat higher, and then put the work in up front. You have to think about trying out a new track to see if it's even better than the one you're on now.

If you've done your homework, and your actions fit your Vision, and you're modeling yourself after the best of the best, and you're working to the best of your ability, then don't worry about being comfortable. If it's the right thing to do, then it doesn't matter whether or not you're comfortable.

The person who can look uncertainty squarely in the eyes and smile will have an awesome life.

You have to control your focus. If I had gone out on that golf course and focused on my outcome of being a great golfer, instead of focusing on the people I thought were watching me, I would have gotten a much better result. If my self-talk had been, "You're doing a great job. You have a nice, calm swing with this great new grip," instead of, "Why do these people have to be here to watch me mess up?" I would have gotten a much better result. And if my physical expression had been one of confidence fueled from an internal source instead of panic taken on from my circumstances, I would have gotten a much better result.

Even though I may have still felt uncomfortable in that moment, by controlling my focus, my self-talk, and my body language, I still would have gotten the result I wanted. The uncomfortable feeling does go away if you persist in going after what you want to the best of your ability and demand great things for yourself. You're the only one who can reset your thermostat. Do it now.

Train It to Trust It

> *""Wipe everything out of your mind but the ball. Glue your eyes to it. Marry it. Nevermind your opponent, the weather, or anything. Make that ball an obsession. If you can get yourself into that trance, pressure won't intrude. It's just you and the ball."*
> — *tennis champion Rod Laver*

Great athletes know that one of the things that separates them from other players is that they trust their mechanisms. They focus their attention on what they want (visualization) and then they trust their unconscious minds to produce that. Once you've trained your mind, you have to trust it. You have to trust that you can make what you want happen under any situation, instead of "over-thinking" the process.

Michael Jordan frequently talked about fundamentals being at the core of success. Fundamentals. Even when he was tired, he trusted his shot and didn't try to overcompensate.

When the moment really counts, championship athletes do the same thing they do in practice. They don't do anything differently. Other people look at a playoff putt or a shot at the buzzer and hold their breath because it's such an important shot. But for the greats, it's just another putt, just another shot. All equal, all the same.

Your unconscious mind doesn't understand the difference between a practice shot and a game-winning shot. You are the only one who can mess that up, by letting your focus, your self-talk, and your physiology run haywire. You've worked hard to put the proper mechanisms in place, and you've worked hard to condition them to respond consistently every time. Now it's time to step outside your comfort zone and trust what you've trained.

Learn to Sky Dive from the Ground

"I got more thrill out of flying before I had ever been in the air at all — while lying in my bed thinking how exciting it would be to fly."
— *Orville Wright*

Remember the unconscious mind? The job of the unconscious mind is to keep your life consistent with what you've experienced in the past, and to make it hard for you to change. To the unconscious mind, it's a matter of survival. You need the unthinking consistency that the unconscious mind provides to run all your vital physical functions; if the unconscious mind didn't do its job, you would die. Celebrate that it's hard to make changes.

But don't let it stop you from consciously choosing to change certain habits, actions and attitudes. Now that you've decided to develop a new identity for yourself, you have to be willing to step into uncertainty. Just like sky diving: that's stepping out and taking a risk. That's being free. But you don't have to sky dive to get the freedom and the feeling that you get when you step out of an airplane, at the mercy of that parachute.

You can capture that exhilaration and those feelings for yourself by stepping up and saying what you need to say to your husband, or to your wife. You can get that by saying "I love you," when you haven't said it in a while. You can get that by apologizing to someone you know you need to apologize to. You can get that by confronting a difficult situation in a way that will empower everyone involved. You can get that by committing that you're going to work out and lose weight and get healthy. You can get that by putting yourself on the line and contributing your time and your energy to a cause larger than yourself. You can get that by supporting someone else in making changes in his own life. And yes, you can get it by imagining "flying" while lying in bed — while imagining exactly who you want to be and what you want to do in your mind.

Do You Have Confidence in Yourself?

"You miss 100% of the shots you never take."
— *Wayne Gretzky*

I remember growing up with a kid who was an outstanding basketball player. Recruiters from all over the country would come to watch him play his game. Everybody was impressed...except him. He never felt he was worthy of his talents. I watched him sabotage himself over and over again. He was his own worst enemy. It really bothered me. One day I got up the courage to ask him why he was wasting his talent. He told me to mind my own business. He had everything he needed to make it big, except a sense of worthiness.

I'm not the most talented guy around, but I've always been a fighter. I'm NOT talking about physical fights; I'm talking about fighting to break the mindset that keeps so many people paralyzed. I'm talking about fighting what other people told me to believe about myself. I respected people's rights to their own opinions, but I fought hard if their opinion threatened to infect me. I fought my limitations every day.

The author Richard Bach said, "Argue hard enough for your limitations, and sure enough, they're yours." Don't argue for your limitations, transcend them. Sometimes it's refreshing to throw a punch at your limitations. I designed my life in my head and then I fought to keep that Vision alive. Most of the time, I have no idea how to do what I've committed to doing, but I don't let that stop me. I didn't wait to start until I've figured everything out. I just keep moving forward, and if I get in my own way then I fight myself. I fight my old identity. I fight my comfort zone.

This is a life-long process. And guess what? Your nervous system wants you to fight for it. If you fight for your Vision, then your unconscious mind and your nervous system know you're serious. That's the key right there. That's what I mean by fight. I don't mean getting into tussles with your neighbors; I mean fighting through Deception and fighting to expand your comfort zone. You have to fight for it.

You May Have to Fight for Your Rights

"Being kind doesn't mean one must be a mat."
                                        — *Maya Angelou*

I read a story that was written in 1911, almost a century ago, and its message is still relevant in our lives today. It's a story about a dog named Sam.

Poor Sam was afraid of everything. His owner was a farmer who hoped Sam would grow out of his cowardliness, but he never did. Sam was a big dog, but he looked puny because he always slunk around with his head down and his tail between his legs.

Every Wednesday, the farmer hitched up the family wagon and rode into town with Sam trailing behind, head down, tail between his legs. All the other dogs in the village snapped at Sam and bit his heels and chased him mercilessly. The farmer was disgusted and embarrassed by his cowardly dog so he decided to take Sam to the pound. When he got home, he tied Sam to a tree, planning to take him the next day. Lucky for Sam, the farmer didn't tie the knot very tight. Sam got loose and took off into the woods. Unluckily for Sam, he fell into a bear trap that the village boys had dug.

Several hours later, along came a bear, and he fell into the pit with Sam. As you can imagine, the bear was NOT happy about this. He took a swipe at Sam and Sam ducked. All Sam wanted was to get away from that bear. There wasn't much room to run, so after the bear chased Sam around the pit a few times for fun, he pounced on him, ready to deliver the finishing blow.

Sam realized that he was about to die. In that moment, something inside Sam came alive and he lunged, teeth bared, at the bear's throat. The bear was thrown back and the fight was on. Sam felt courage for the first time in his life and he wasn't about to give in.

When the boys came by to check their trap in the morning, they found Sam and the bear on opposite sides of the pit, growling at each other but keeping their distance.

The boys shot the bear and lifted Sam out of the pit. He was pretty torn up, but he had survived. The boys took him back to the farmer who decided Sam deserved a second chance, and nursed him back to health.

After a few weeks of recovery, Sam was well enough to go with the farmer on his Wednesday trip. As soon as the other dogs of the village saw him, they rushed up to bite him just like they always had. But this time, Sam was having none of it. He lunged at them, growling, just as he had lunged at the bear. They dogs ran home yelping. They weren't about to take on this dog who could obviously take care of himself.

After that, he was top dog. When Sam had realized his life was on the line and he stood up to the bear, he found courage in himself he never knew he had. Now, Sam walks with confidence; his head held high and his tail straight up.

Standing up and fighting for yourself doesn't mean you have to hurt people or hurt yourself. Standing up and fighting for something just means that you've developed a certain amount of determination and intensity towards achieving your goal. And that's something you need to decide for yourself.

Sometimes you need to fight for higher standards, for the right to be left alone in peace, for more joy. When you believe in yourself enough not to let other people knock you down, you force them to treat you with the respect you want, need, and deserve. You're living life like you belong here — without apology and without letting other people take advantage of you. When you carry yourself with a strong presence, when you tower instead of cower, people will sense your confidence and will treat you accordingly.

You don't have to be aggressive. The other dogs didn't change the way they responded to Sam because he fought the bear; they changed because of the way Sam carried himself after he fought the bear. Sam's fight with the bear simply showed him that he had courage all the time; he just needed to call upon it. Sam's story is about carrying yourself with the conviction that you are a person who belongs here and is worthy of respect.

Your bear might be that you were assaulted or molested. Your bear might be that you grew up poor. Your bear might be that you're failing in school or in business. Your bear might be being picked on and ridiculed. Everybody has his or her own "bear" in life. If you've faced your bear, and you're still here, be proud of yourself and carry yourself with that pride. Just like Sam.

Are You Ready for the Bottom Line?

"Good-bye is always hello to something else.
Good-bye / hello, good-bye / hello, like the sound of a
rocking chair."
— *George Ella Lyons*

Take a look at the different areas of your life. If you want an intimate relationship, but don't have one, you're in your comfort zone and you've been unwilling to step out of it. If your intimate relationship isn't as intimate as you'd like, you're in your comfort zone and you've been unwilling to step out of it. If you don't have the career you want, you're in your comfort zone and you've been unwilling to step out of it. If you don't have the energy and the vitality that you want, you're in your comfort zone and you've been unwilling to step out of it. For every area of your life, if it's not where you want it to be, then you're in your comfort zone and you've been unwilling to step out of it. Bottom line.

But now, you have no excuses. You know exactly what to do and how to do it. It's time to step out of your comfort zone and take some risks. It's time to find out who you really are and who you are capable of becoming. You have to. You must. We have amazing potential, but we're not using it if we're unwilling to step out of the comfort zones that we've created for ourselves. Stop holding onto attitudes and ways of thinking that aren't working. Stop holding onto habits and actions that don't serve your life.

It truly comes down to understanding that life is about the journey: the hard times and the bad times and the good times and the joyful times. All of that put together is who we are. We can find just as much joy in the hard times as we can in the great times if we have the right mindset, if we take everything that happens in our life and use it to make ourselves better.

And you have to realize that you're worthy of it; you're worthy of the gold medal in life. I want you to know, too, that if you're going through a program like this, that says to me that you have a high Performance Quotient. I don't know about your IQ, but I know you have a high PQ. Maybe you haven't been perfect in following this program, but I know that you've accomplished something great. Congratulations. And this is just the beginning. So step outside of your comfort zone. Make it happen for yourself and realize that you are full of possibilities, and that you always have been.

Understand the Gratitude Quadrant

"Gratitude is the sign of noble souls."

— Aesop

As we wrap up this book, I want to share one woman's question. She asked, "I agree with everything you've said, but don't we ever just stop and relax and be content with what we have or who we are? Are we supposed to always keep changing?"

Great question. It gave me an opportunity to share what I call The Gratitude Quadrant. I believe it's important to be grateful, but we don't want to become content. You see, contentment is defined as being so satisfied with what we have, that we have no motivation to get better. Contentment can lead to stagnation.

On the other hand, we can be grateful for everything that is right with our life, and still want to improve. Our desire for more doesn't mean we don't appreciate what we have; it's just based on our belief that human beings are meant to grow.

I've come to understand there are four ways to approach life. We are either:

A. Grateful and Satisfied (We like things just the way they are, and feel no compulsion to change.)

B. Ungrateful and Dissatisfied (We don't like our life, but we're trying to improve it.)

C. Grateful and Dissatisfied (We appreciate what's right in our life, and are taking action to make it even better.)

D. Ungrateful and Satisfied (We are unhappy with our life, but we're not doing anything to improve it.)

Which quadrant best describes your outlook? Most of us tend to have a consistent way of looking at life-while some of us have different outlooks for different parts of our life. I know one man who is Quadrant A with his work and Quadrant D with his weight. He works for the government and really likes the monthly paycheck and the pension plan that will be waiting for him when he retires — but he is always complaining about being out of shape and yet never does anything about it.

Perfectionists are permanently locked in Quadrant B. They don't like themselves, and they're always trying to get better, but they are never able to measure up to their impossible standards, so they never get to a state of gratitude. They live in a perpetual state of dissatisfaction.

I believe it is in our best interest to be in Quadrant C in all areas of our life. That way, we live in a state of gratitude in which we recognize everything that's going well, and yet we are constructively trying to do more, be more, and have more. My young son is a marvelous example of Quadrant C. He loves life, and yet he is always eager to try new things and learn new skills. In many ways, he's my hero.

Your Future Is in Your Hands

"Every exit is an entry somewhere else."
                                                    — *Tom Stoppard*

It is my sincere hope that this book will be your ticket into the quality of life you've always wanted. Please don't put this book up on a shelf. Keep it out on your nightstand or on your desk where you'll see it frequently. Pick it up and review your underlined notes. Reread a few pages and ask yourself whether you're following up on what you've learned. Hold yourself accountable for incorporating these principles into your life. Review the "Try

This at Home" section at the end of each chapter so you continue to put these ideas into practice.

Now, go out, take the challenge, and make your life what you want it to be — today, not someday.

Try This at Home —
Questions, Suggestions, and Action Plans

To Explore

- In which areas of your life are you still a Reactor or Stagnator?
- Why is it important that you identify those areas?
- What will you gain by changing into a Proactor?
- What will it cost you in your life if you choose to remain a Reactor or Stagnator?
- If the ultimate Proactor looked at your life, what changes would he say are needed?
- What changes are you committed to making in your life?

To Act

- Create a record of your goals, lessons learned, and accomplishments.
- Record your progress every day for 45 days.
- Celebrate your successes.

To Remember

- Unseen forces are working to help bring you what you want in life when you do your part to the best of your ability.

Now What?

As promised in the beginning of the book, I'm happy to share more about The 45 Day Challenge® with you. The 45 Day Challenge® is significant to our core training philosophy: In order to create lasting change and growth for the long term, not just a day, week or month, you need to align your identity with the thoughts and habits that support who you want to be and where you want to go. This philosophy applies to all of our clients-- corporate executives, leaders and team members. And more importantly, it applies to *you*!

The 45 Day Challenge® series includes: The 45 Day Challenge® for Life Balance, The 45 Day Challenge® to Sales Mastery, The 45 Day Challenge® to Outstanding Leadership, The 45 Day Challenge® for Entrepreneurs, and The 45 Day Challenge® for Youth Leadership. Each 45 Day Challenge® course is designed to align your desired identity with supporting habits in four key areas. For example, in The 45 Day Challenge® for Life Balance, you will align your habits to the identity you desire for your mind-set, your health/energy, your relationships, and your career.

The theory behind the 45 days is simple. Studies show that it takes 21-40 days to break or build a habit. We take you through a 45 day process to instill the habits and principles you've read about in this book. We will guide you through the change process, which we call the Cycle of Performance: Inception, Deception, Transformation, and Identity as you grow to another level and new identity.

For 45 days, 30 minutes a day, you are guided through a personal on-line course (or playbook), which you can do from home or at work, to align your desired identity with the habits that will support it. You will be guided to think about and take specific actions each day. The program is broken down in 6 weeks; each week you will graduate to a new level. For example, in The 45 Day Challenge® for Life Balance, Week 1 will have you creating new visions and goals for your life in four distinct areas. At the end of the week, you will earn the title of Visionary Master. In Week 2 you'll be breaking unwanted habits by identifying the habits in your life that don't support your new visions and replacing those habits with new ones. You'll also get a chance to create habit-interrupts as we call them. At the end of the week you will learn how to become a Habit Breaker and so on...

Another element that makes this program so unique is that we provide you with the accountability support necessary to keep you focused for 45 days. People from all over the country and from many different companies are taking any given Challenge right along with you. You will be placed on a small cyber-team and be able communicate and support each other via email. You will have an advisor that will hold you accountable to your goals and visions for yourself, support you through Deception, and send you daily emails of encouragement and inspiration. Your team will have a live conference call with a certified Envision U coach once a week for thirty minutes (afternoon and evening calls offered) when you'll learn what to focus on for the week ahead.

Can The 45 Day Challenge® Help Me?

"The five most dangerous words in the English language are, 'Maybe it will go away'."
— sign in a dentist's office

Here are just a few stories from people like you who initially wondered if committing to The 45 Day Challenge® program would pay off for them:

Meet Debbie

A CEO colleague, Debbie, shared a concern, "I'm the incoming president of a professional association. I know how to motivate employees, but I'm kind of rusty on how to manage volunteers who don't count on me for a paycheck. Can your 45 Day Challenge® help me with that?"

I reassured her that The Challenge does address how to become a more effective leader, and shared some of the bottom-line results other participants have produced as a result of their involvement. She decided to sign up.

Six months later she reported back, "The Challenge helped me rethink my patterns of communication and build better relationships with my volunteers. I'm noticing gradual improvements even beyond my role as association president. I've relearned how to listen and incorporate ideas from other people, instead of wanting to do everything myself. One of my managers even complimented me on it the other day. An added bonus is that my family likes me better, too."

Meet Dave

Another manager named Dave was very frustrated at work. He told me, "No matter what I do, I just can't get my team to work together. It seems like every day is filled with personality conflicts. Any suggestions?"

I suggested he go through The 45 Day Challenge® to Outstanding Leadership. I told him it would fit easily into his schedule and would help him acquire the ability to influence and motivate his employees to work together more cooperatively. Before he was halfway through the Challenge, Dave started noticing improvements in his team. By the end of the 45 days, his staff was coming to him with ideas on how they could be even more productive. As he proudly said, "A complete turnaround!"

Meet Kathy

Kathy, a working mother, was feeling overwhelmed by the multiple demands of her family and her job. She confided, "There are days when I feel like I'm not doing anything right. Sometimes, I just want to run away from everything."

I knew The 45 Day Challenge® for Life Balance could help her, but she was understandably reluctant to add another "to do" to her already packed schedule. I asked, "Kathy, will things improve in the next 45 days if you don't do something differently?" She realized she had to take action or she'd continue to feel overwhelmed. That simple question helped her understand that her problems wouldn't go away on their own—she needed to summon the courage to confront them. I reassured her that she wouldn't have to go at it alone and that she'd have plenty of support from our Envision U advisors. She agreed to try it.

During our final conference coaching call, Kathy couldn't stop thanking me. She said she had grown so much as a person, parent, and professional, and that she now felt more in control of her life. She said her family life was incredible and that she was tremendously grateful. I told her she had done all the work; The Challenge was only her guide.

Meet Ed

In case you're wondering, these ideas can also help you become a better partner. Just looking at Ed, one of my clients, I could tell something was wrong. He admitted sadly, "My wife and I aren't getting along. We're thinking of getting a divorce." Ed had heard about The 45 Day Challenge® from co-workers and wanted to know if it could help save his marriage.

I told Ed that The Challenge had helped many couples learn how to communicate better, which helped them start growing in the same direction. This often recreated the affection and mutual respect that brought them together in the first place.

"We've never been happier together!" Ed burst out when I saw him several months later. He said, "I would have called you sooner, but we've been traveling. The Challenge saved our marriage. Thank you!"

Does the Challenge Produce Bottom-Line Results?

"I like things to happen, and if they don't happen, I like to make them happen."

— *Winston Churchill*

Meet Brad

A father named Brad called with some general questions about our program. I sensed he had a "hidden agenda" that was bothering him. After talking for a few minutes, he finally got down to the real issue. "I've got to get a raise," he said anxiously. "One of my kids starts college next year, and we're barely paying our bills now. I don't know how I'm going to be able to afford the tuition. Can The 45 Day Challenge® help me?"

I shared some of these success stories with him and let him know that many of our graduates tell us this has been the best investment they've ever made in themselves. He thought about it for a few days and then called back to register for our next Challenge.

"I can hardly believe the changes," he told me shortly after completing the program. "I asked for and was given a small raise. More importantly, I stopped making myself the only one in charge of our family spending. I've started sharing responsibility with my wife and kids so they're more accountable for smart spending. They're making good choices—and they're learning from all of it. We talk more. We even laugh more. The kids' growing maturity has surprised and pleased me. I'll use this process again."

Meet Kim

A saleswoman named Kim left an email on our website saying she wanted to sign up for our next Challenge. "I'm in a sales slump. I was a top producer for three years running. Now, for some reason, I seem to have lost the magic. A friend told me your program boosted his sales by 23%. I need your help!"

Kim said in her follow-up evaluation, "The 45 Day Challenge® for Sales Mastery showed me that I had been neglecting many of the productive habits that had made me successful in the first place. I've had some personal setbacks, so I had stopped doing what worked and started taking the easy way out. It was initially hard regaining those good habits, but as soon as I returned to the healthy behaviors that had worked for me in the beginning, my sales and life both started improving. This time I'll stop myself *before* I go into a slide and keep my resolve to aim high."

Are You Ready to Take the Challenge?

"Is there ever any particular spot where one can put one's finger and say, 'It all began that day, at such a time, and such a place, with such an incident'?"
— Agatha Christie

I'm not making outrageous claims. These people did not become millionaires overnight. They did not marry royalty or instantly lose 40 pounds.

They did something more important than that. They discovered, or rediscovered, their power to produce lasting positive change. They acquired, or re-acquired, the transforming ability to attain meaningful goals while enjoying more ease in their lives. The good news for you is that the ideas you've read about in this book have helped thousands of people from all walks of life produce similar results in the last ten years.

These people include: an executive who accelerated his rise from sales manager to CEO in five years; a trainer of Olympic athletes who used what she learned about mindset to help her gymnast clients win medals; a martial arts master who credits the program with helping him develop new levels of performance and contentment; and a father whose new habits helped him reconnect with his three children after returning from a long, overseas work assignment.

You can benefit just as they did. Do you want to live a richer, fuller life? Do you want to contribute more to your family, community, profession, and world? Do you feel you have untapped reserves of talent and skill? Do you know there are disturbing shadows in your life that are preventing you from being the healthy, happy parent, spouse, friend, and citizen you could be? If you know any of these things, then it's time for you to take the first step toward becoming the person you want to be.

Look at your calendar. Note today's date. Count 45 days from today and put a big star on that date. Isn't it wonderful to know that if you start taking action today, you will have tangibly improved your quality of life by that date? That is my promise to you. And I am here to help and support you along the way. A new 45 Day Challenge® begins almost every month. You may sign up for the next 45 Day Challenge® and get more information by visiting our website www.envision-u.com, emailing us at info@envision-u.com, or calling us at 800-684-5248.

Once again, I have thoroughly enjoyed sharing the principles of The 45 Day Challenge® in this book. I hope you have found them interesting and useful. Make your life what you want it to be—now, not someday!

Rod

We Want to Hear from You!

"The purpose of life isn't to be happy; it's to matter, to feel it has made some difference that you have lived at all."

— *Leo Rosten*

Have you made positive changes as a result of reading this book? Do you have a success story you'd like to share with others so they can learn from your example? Have you run into an obstacle or challenge that you would like to be addressed on our website or in our next book? We encourage you to take a few moments and send in your ideas, questions, and real-life examples of how the information in this book has impacted you.

If you're interested in having Rod or an Envision U Coach speak at your next conference or train your staff please call us at 800-684-5248. We'll be happy to answer your questions about availability and how we can tailor these ideas to your association members and staff.

We'd love to hear from you!